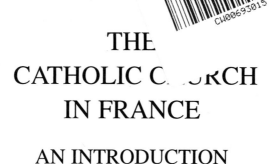

THE CATHOLIC C. ..RCH IN FRANCE

AN INTRODUCTION

Roger Greenacre

THE COUNCIL FOR CHRISTIAN UNITY
OF THE GENERAL SYNOD OF THE CHURCH OF ENGLAND

 Occasional Paper No. 4

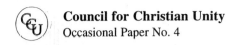

Council for Christian Unity
Occasional Paper No. 4

Signed occasional papers are published by the Council for Christian Unity in the belief that their contents are likely to prove of interest, but any opinions expressed are not necessarily those of the Council.

ISBN 0 7151 5752 3

First published in 1996 by the Council for Christian Unity of the General Synod of the Church of England.

Copyright of Illustrations

Front cover, p.27: A. Pinoges/CIRIC

p.iii: R. Taurines/CIRIC

pp.4,6,13: Bibliothèque Nationale

p.16: Archive of John XXIII

p.23: P. Dupin/CIRIC

p.36: P. Leprince/CIRIC

p.47: Church Commissioners (photograph: Courtauld Institute of Art)

Acknowledgement

Grateful thanks are due also to the following for their help with illustrations: Pierre Janin; *Unité Chrétienne,* Lyon; Suzanne Martineau; Monastère de Chevetogne; Claudie Perreau; *Unité des Chrétiens*; Janet Mellor and the editors of *Ave*; Denys Allanore; Abbaye Notre-Dame du Bec.

Front cover: *Messe pour la France. Outside Notre-Dame-de-Paris on the occasion of a national celebration. From left to right: Mgr Duval, Archbishop of Rouen (now President of the French Episcopal Conference); the late Cardinal Decourtray, Archbishop of Lyon; Cardinal Lustiger, Archbishop of Paris; Mgr Vilnet, Bishop of Lille.*

Printed in England by Bourne Press Ltd

Pope John Paul II concelebrating at Paray-le Monial (Diocese of Autun) in 1986 with three of his fellow bishops. From left to right: the late Cardinal Decourtray, Archbishop of Lyon, Mgr Le Bourgeois, then Bishop of Autun, and Mgr Vilnet, Bishop of Lille and then President of the French Episcopal Conference

CONTENTS

FOREWORD

France is among England's closest neighbours, and contacts between the two countries are intensive and increasing. Many English people live in France and many more take holidays or even maintain second homes there. Indeed, it is now even possible to live in France and commute to work in England, or vice versa. Not surprisingly, the Church of England and the Church in France have similarly enjoyed a longstanding relationship. Today, there are intensive contacts between Anglicans and Roman Catholics within France; five Anglican dioceses in England are linked with a diocese in France, and there are numerous parish links, or civic links in which the churches participate. For all those involved in such cross-channel relationships this book will be an essential resource.

Its publication will also point to and, I hope, strengthen the Church of England's commitment to all-round ecumenism. At a time when unity between the Church of England and its Lutheran neighbours across the North Sea is receiving much attention, it is particularly important to strengthen our relationships with the Roman Catholic Church across the Channel as well as within England. I pray that the story of the long-standing and close friendship between the Church of England and the Roman Catholic Church in France told in these pages will encourage us all to work for even closer fellowship and deeper unity. Recently, the Church of England has also entered into Conversations with the French Lutheran and Reformed Churches. They will be the subject of a future publication.

No one in the Church of England is better qualified to write such a book than Canon Roger Greenacre. His knowledge of the French Church is unequalled among English Anglicans, and he has personally played a very important role in the blossoming of relations between the two churches during the last thirty years. For this, as for the present book, we owe him a great debt of gratitude.

✠ DAVID GRIMSBY

Chairman, Council for Christian Unity   *26 September 1995*

iv

INTRODUCTION

This book does not arise from any personal initiative on my part, but results from an invitation from the Council for Christian Unity to write a booklet on the Roman Catholic Church in France as a sequel to Colin Podmore's *The German Evangelical Churches: An Introduction* (1992). It has very limited aims; it is intended to provide a readership envisaged as coming, in the first place, from the ranks of English Anglicans with an introduction to the Roman Catholic Church in France – its history, its present life and mission and its particular relations with the Church of England. For this reason the Anglican presence in France is evoked only so far as is necessary to tell the story of Anglican - French Roman Catholic relations. Similarly, French Protestantism and the Church in Belgium are only brought into the story in order to illuminate its main themes; both deserve to be the subject of separate publications. I have decided to use the title *The Catholic Church in France*, since that is how it is known by the other churches and ecclesial communities in France. The expression 'Roman Catholic' is almost unknown in French and is hardly ever used except in translations of dialogue texts involving Anglicans.

I am grateful to the Diocese of Chichester and my colleagues on the Administrative Chapter of Chichester Cathedral for allowing me two months' sabbatical leave in 1993 and to the Council for Christian Unity for a financial grant towards that sabbatical. Many people have helped me with the preparation and production of this book. It is impossible to name them all, and I refrain from naming some whose comments were made to me on the understanding that they would not be attributed. I can, however, acknowledge with gratitude help received from the Archbishop of Birmingham, the Bishop of Cahors, the Abbot of Bec, the Abbé Eric Aumonier, Père Guillaume de Bertier de Sauvigny, Prof. Frank Bowman, the Abbé Patrick Chauvet, Soeur Marguerite Delmotte, the Abbé Louis Derousseaux, the Venerable Martin Draper, Archdeacon of France, Mrs Pamela Gaughan, Mr Robert Gray, Mr Peter Harvey, Canon Jeremy Haselock, Edme and Daniela Jeanson, M. le Chanoine François Legaux, Mr Harold Mandeville, Mrs Margot Mayne, Mlle Suzanne Martineau, M. Bruno Neveu, the Abbé Pierre Parré, M. le Chanoine Arnoldus van der Westhuizen Smit, Bertrand and Jane Saint-Sernin, the Revd Dr Kenneth Stevenson, Dr Mary Tanner, Soeur Vincenette d'Uzer and M. Alain Woodrow. I should also like to thank all the other members of the Belgian, English and French ARCs (Anglican - Roman Catholic Committees) and of the Council for Christian Unity, together with Mrs Louise Matcham, Canons' Secretary at Chichester Cathedral, the Consulate-General of the British Embassy in Paris and the French Embassy in London. A very special word of thanks must go to Dr Colin Podmore, without whose warm encouragement and patient but firmly persistent editorial oversight the work would never have been begun and would most certainly never have been completed this side of the *Parousia*.

ROGER GREENACRE   *25 August (St Louis, King of France) 1995*

MAP OF THE DIOCESES OF FRANCE

Archiepiscopal sees are in capitals, others in lower case.

Reproduced, with permission, from the 1995 edition of *L'Eglise Catholique en France* (Conférence des Evêques de France)

I THE ELDEST DAUGHTER OF THE CHURCH

The Beginnings

If France has at times boasted of her privileged position with regard to the Church in somewhat exaggerated language, calling herself *'la fille aînée de l'Eglise'* (the eldest daughter of the Church) and her king *Rex Christianissimus* (the Most Christian King), it is nonetheless true that the history of the Church in France goes back at least to the second century. The martyrdom of Pothinus, Bishop of Lyon, with Blandina and others in the year 177 is well attested, and the successor of St Pothinus was none other than St Irenaeus. He came from Asia Minor and had known St Polycarp, Bishop of Smyrna, who, it is claimed, had been a disciple of the Apostle John. To this day, the Archbishop of Lyon bears the title of *Primat des Gaules* (Primate of the Gauls), though it is now purely honorific. The Church in Gaul, which by the year 300 had at least 25 bishops, produced a number of notable figures, among them St Hilary of Poitiers (d. 367), 'the Athanasius of the West', and his disciple St Martin of Tours (d. 397). The latter founded the first monastery in Gaul – Ligugé, near Poitiers (now a Benedictine Abbey) – and was the first monk in the West to become a bishop. The Gauls were overrun by the Franks, and it was only when the Frankish king, Clovis, was baptized at Reims by St Remigius that the future of the Church seemed secure.[1] By the sixth century it had fourteen provinces with 100 bishops. Among those who played a prominent role as missionaries or educators among the Franks were the Irishman St Columbanus (d. 615) and Alcuin of York (d. 804), 'the Schoolmaster of Europe'.

The Middle Ages

To the mediaeval Church France made two major positive contributions. The first was a dominant role in the development of monasticism, a history marked by the reforms of St Benedict of Aniane (d. 821), the foundation of Cluny (909) and nearly two centuries later that of the Cistercian Order (1098), whose survival and popularization were assured by St Bernard of Clairvaux (1090-1153). Both Cluny and the Cistercians were to found monasteries all over Europe, and Cluny was to be an important influence in the eleventh-century reform of the Papacy. Among other new monastic creations in France in the eleventh and twelfth centuries was the Carthusian Order, which was brought to England by St Hugh (c.1140-1200), later to become Bishop of Lincoln. The second contribution was a no less dominant role in the intellectual and theological life of the Church and in the rise of the universities. These had their precursors in the eleventh and twelfth centuries in the cathedral and monastic schools, such as the School of Chartres and the School of Bec under Lanfranc (c.1010-1089) and Anselm (c.1033-1109) – two true Europeans, both of whom were born in Italy, became monks in Normandy and

---

[1] The date traditionally ascribed to this event is 496; the Church in France is trying to seize the opportunity of celebrating its fifteenth centenary for re-launching its mission to the people of France.

1

ended up as Archbishops of Canterbury; it found its solid base in the earliest of the northern universities, Paris. At the turning point between the twelfth and thirteenth centuries Paris was indeed the intellectual capital of Western Europe; 70 per cent of the teaching body at the University were foreigners. A crucial and formative role in this history was played by Peter Abelard (1079-1142), whose influence on the development of the dialectical method in the teaching of philosophy and theology was crucial.

Ecclesia Gallicana

Other contributions from France to the life of the mediaeval Church were more ambivalent. In this category can be included a leading role in the Crusades, and the fact that the two major early challenges to mediaeval Catholic orthodoxy, though very different from each other, found their main focus in France – the Waldensians in Lyon and the Cathars or Albigensians in Languedoc. Most important of all was the fourteenth-century 'Babylonian Captivity' of the Papacy in Avignon (though, to be fair, anarchy and civil war in Rome itself were largely to blame for the move of the Bishops of Rome to Avignon). Politically, Avignon did not become part of France until the French Revolution, but the Avignon Papacy was only too evidently under strong pressure from the Kings of France and, at the time of the Hundred Years' War between England and France, this led to a certain disaffection towards the Papacy in England and legislation in the English Parliament that anticipated some of the measures later taken by Henry VIII. Later, with the Western Church divided between rival Popes at Rome and at Avignon (and even for a time among three Popes), it was from the University of Paris that was elaborated a 'conciliarist' theology, which – by arguing for the superiority of the General Council over the Pope – would allow the Council of Constance to end the schism in 1417.

It was in the University of Paris that the school of theology which came to be known as *Gallicanism* was born: it asserted both the more or less complete freedom of the French Church, *Ecclesia Gallicana*, from papal control and also the superiority of the Council over the Pope. Although, after the ending of the Schism, the Popes fought hard against conciliarism, they did so by gaining favour with powerful monarchies through a series of separate agreements or concordats. Already, by the Pragmatic Sanction of Bourges in 1438, the Kings of France were granted the right of nomination to the principal sees; this privilege became more general with the Concordat of 1516 which gave the King the right to nominate not only to all bishoprics but also to abbacies. The institution of 'commendatory' abbots, who were not themselves monks, had a devastating effect on monastic life. It was the phenomenon of boy abbots at the French Court – younger sons of aristocratic families in most cases – that led to the custom of clerics being generally addressed as 'Monsieur l'Abbé' (Abbot), since courtiers could safely assume that adolescent ecclesiastics at court, though not yet ordained, would enjoy the title and revenue of at least one abbacy.

The Protestant Reformation made a strong appeal in France, and the outstanding systematic theologian of the sixteenth-century Reformation, Jean Calvin, was a Frenchman, though he was destined to spend most of his life in Geneva. France was devastated by fierce and bloody religious civil war, only brought to an end when the Protestant ('Huguenot') leader Henri de Navarre became King Henri IV of France. He had first become a Roman Catholic ('Paris vaut bien une messe' – Paris is well worth a mass), but then provided a measure of toleration for his Protestant subjects by the Edict of Nantes in 1598.

The seventeenth century – *le grand siècle* – was a particularly important period, brilliant but troubled, for the Church in France, as for the Church of England. It took at least half a century for the decrees of the reforming Council of Trent to be finally accepted in France and longer for them to be put into effect, but a number of outstanding reformers and saints worked to transform the life of the Church,[2] all of whom were to have an influence far beyond the frontiers of France. This century was also to see the planting of the Church in Canada, thanks to the heroic missionary efforts of the Jesuits, many of whom died as martyrs.

'The Most Christian King' Louis XIV was to intervene as personally and as dictatorially in the life of the French Church as the Tudors in England. He revoked Henri IV's Edict of Nantes in 1685 and persecuted *'la Religion Prétendue Réformée'* (the so-called Reformed Religion), so causing vast numbers of Huguenots to flee abroad; they were to make a significant contribution to the cultural and economic life of the countries (among them England) in which they settled. He also repressed Jansenism. This was a movement of theology and spirituality named after Cornelius Jansen, Bishop of Ypres (1585-1638) and centred on the Abbey of Port-Royal, whose conflict with the Jesuits over its theology of grace (inspired by St Augustine) led to accusations of neo-Calvinism and to condemnation by Rome. It attracted the support of such notable laymen as the philosopher Blaise Pascal and the playwright Jean Racine and was in part responsible for the beginnings of Old Catholicism in Utrecht. Finally, notwithstanding considerable papal opposition, he reinforced his own control over the Gallican Church. The high point of this latter campaign came in 1682 with the promulgation by the Assembly of the French Clergy (a body of bishops and priests similar to the English Convocations) of the Four Gallican Articles drawn up by Jacques-Bénigne Bossuet (1627-1704), the redoubtable Bishop of Meaux and one of the most noted preachers of the age. These denied all authority to the Pope in the temporal concerns of nation states, upheld the decrees of the Council of Constance affirming the supremacy of General Councils over the Pope, reaffirmed the 'liberties of the Gallican Church' (as they were called), and declared that the judgements of the Pope were not irreformable until confirmed by a General Council.

---

[2] Among them were bishops such as St François de Sales (1567-1622), François de Salignac de la Mothe Fénelon (1651-1715) and Bossuet (1627-1704) and reformers of the priestly life and founders of new religious congregations such as Cardinal de Bérulle (1575-1629), M. Olier (1608-57), St Jean Eudes (1601-80), St Vincent de Paul (c. 1580-1660), St Jeanne-Françoise de Chantal (1572-1641) and St Louise de Marillac (1591-1660).

Although Louis XIV ceded to pressure from Rome and officially withdrew these Articles some eleven years later, they did not cease to have considerable influence in France; it remained the case until the French Revolution that no papal bulls or encyclicals could be put into practice in France until registered by the Paris *Parlement* and no national or regional synod be held without the King's authorization. As late as 1766 a commission with full powers to reform the religious orders was established by royal authority without reference to Rome.

JACQUES BENIGNE BOSSUET

Evesque de Meaux.

The French Revolution

To understand France it is necessary to realize the radical break in continuity in the life of the nation, its structures and mentality, caused by the French Revolution, an event moreover that was to influence the whole of Europe (at least of Western Europe) and to arouse extremes both of hope and fear even in countries like England which were not to experience its effects at first hand. Moreover, the divisions caused in France by the Revolution were to affect very directly the life of the Church right up to modern times.

Although the Revolution had been prepared for intellectually by an 'Enlightenment' hostile to institutional Christianity and dominated by Voltaire and Rousseau, in its first phase in 1789 a majority of the clergy represented in the States General actively supported the movement for reform. This was particularly true of the lower clergy, who were themselves alienated from the bishops, not only on account of their great wealth but because access to the episcopate had come to be reserved almost exclusively to members of the aristocracy. Revolutionary changes included the confiscation of all church properties, the sale of many of them and the suppression of the monasteries. The really crucial turning point, however, came with the Civil Constitution of the Clergy of 1790. This radically reorganized the dioceses (to correspond with the new *départements*), provided for the popular election (by all enfranchised voters) of bishops and *curés* (who were now state employees), and forbad any bishop-elect to seek confirmation from the Pope, requiring him instead simply to write to him 'in order to witness to the unity of faith and communion he must maintain with him'. The hostile reaction of the bishops and of the Pope only hardened the attitude of the National Assembly, which now prescribed an oath of loyalty to the Constitution, with deprivation of office for all who refused. This led to a schism in the French Church between what came to be called the Constitutional Church, which the Pope condemned as endangering the unity of the Church and which was accepted by only four of the diocesan bishops (the most notable of whom was Talleyrand, Bishop of Autun) and about a third of the clergy, and the *insermentés* or non-jurors, whose clergy were soon forced to choose between exile and going underground, thereby risking imprisonment and, later, martyrdom. In three bloody days at the beginning of September 1792 three bishops and over 225 priests were slaughtered in Paris by the revolutionary mob. This was followed in the next year by a popular uprising in the staunchly Catholic Vendée and its savage suppression. In view of the initially favourable attitude of so many French Catholics to the movement of reform promised by the Revolution and of the prevalence among them of Gallican ideas, it is highly significant that the great majority of them displayed a firm attachment of faith to the See of Rome as the centre and focus of Catholic unity and a willingness to resist to the point of exile or martyrdom. The Revolution soon manifested unconditional hostility to the Christian faith, and in this next wave of persecution the Constitutional Church also suffered, for although 23 of its bishops denied the faith and nine of them married, eight of them went to the guillotine. By the summer of 1794 it looked as if Christianity was now extinct in France. Indeed, the situation began to deteriorate elsewhere on the Continent, as the effects of the French Revolution spread. The frail and octogenarian Pope Pius VI was arrested by the French in Rome in 1798; he died a prisoner in France at Valence the following year and was given a secular funeral by the Republic.

The Napoleonic Concordat of 1801

In 1799 a *coup d'état* brought Napoleon Bonaparte to power; the fate of the French Church was now in the hands of an overwhelmingly powerful personality who can be seen with some justice as both its 'saviour' and its 'gaoler'. The Church, however, was to find an able and skilled protagonist in the new Pope, Pius VII. He was to suffer many defeats and humiliations in his long struggle with Napoleon, but he was nonetheless able to set the French Church on the road to recovery, although the price that had to be paid was heavy. Napoleon's basic motivation was political; he realized that in trying to create peace, stability and harmony in France it was essential to solve the religious question and so restore the Catholic Church to something of its former position, without going so far as to alienate the partisans of the Revolution. The result was the Concordat of 1801, which was to govern Church-State relationships for a century and which is, even today, their basis in Alsace-Lorraine.

The Concordat was necessarily a compromise, with concessions wrung from a reluctant Pope and with ambiguous consequences for the life of the Church. On the whole the main lines of the 1516 Concordat were followed, except that Catholicism was now no longer the religion of the State but that of 'the great majority of French citizens', so confirming and formalizing the recognized status which had been accorded earlier to the Protestants and the Jews. The Napoleonic passion for centralized state control affected every aspect of French society. It was not only within the Church that this was resented,

SIGNATURE DU CONCORDAT.

Entre le Gouvernemant Français et sa Sainteté Pie VII. Pour le rétablißement du Culte Catholique en France.

A contemporary print of the signing of the Concordat. Joseph Bonaparte (third from left) signs for his brother, Napoleon.

but it was the State's rigid grip of the educational system which provoked an inevitable conflict with the Church, which was to prove a running sore in Church-State relations throughout the nineteenth century and into the twentieth. The most radical provision, however – one which in the long run was to strengthen the Ultramontanes (or Papalists) over the Gallicans – was the simple abolition by a stroke of the pen of all the dioceses of pre-revolutionary France (more than 130 in number) and their replacement by 60 new dioceses, together with the Papal demand that all the bishops of the *ancien régime* must resign their sees. The new episcopate did indeed include sixteen of these bishops, translated to new sees; it also included twelve bishops of the Constitutional Church, who made their peace with Rome and so brought that particular schism to an end. A new schism however – *la Petite-Eglise* – came into being, for of the 93 survivors of the original episcopate 38 refused to recognize the Pope's right to suppress their sees and require their resignation. Some of them kept up their resistance to the end (but without consecrating successors), the last of them, Mgr de Thémines, Bishop of Blois, maintaining stubbornly that he was the sole legitimate bishop of the Church of France. The see of Blois illustrates the complexity of the divisions in the French Church at the time, since Henri Grégoire, who took possession of the diocese (Loir-et-Cher) during the Revolution and resigned it at the time of the Concordat, was the only one of the former leaders of the Constitutional Church publicly to maintain his radical political and ecclesiastical convictions to the end. After the death of Mgr de Thémines in 1829 *la Petite-Eglise* no longer had any bishops, and it has had no priests since 1847; nevertheless it still maintains a shadowy existence in one or two pockets of resistance, with around 4,500 adherents.

The Revolution and the Concordat

To give a concrete example, the present diocese of Coutances (officially the Diocese of Coutances and Avranches) in Normandy is the result of the 1801 Concordat which united the two separate dioceses of Coutances and Avranches, a fusion anticipated by the 1791 Civil Constitution. The Constitutional Bishop of the Manche (for the Constitutional bishops took their official title from the *département* rather than from a city) was, after reconciliation with Rome, appointed Bishop of Valence in 1802, and in the same year a new bishop was appointed and consecrated for the Diocese of Coutances. The dispossessed pre-Revolutionary Bishop of Coutances had died in exile in London in 1798; the last Bishop of Avranches, who died in London in 1808, was among those who refused the Pope's demand that they should resign their sees; however, in a gesture of conciliation and to avoid schism, he appointed the new Bishop of Coutances as his Vicar-General. The pre-Revolutionary Bishops of Coutances claimed jurisdiction over the Channel Islands, but when the new Diocese was formed in 1801 to coincide with the boundaries of the Manche the Channel Islands were 'forgotten'. It is now the Roman Catholic Bishop of Portsmouth who exercises jurisdiction over Roman Catholics in the islands.

Although Pius VII came to Paris for the imperial coronation of Napoleon in 1804, this was not enough to prevent a breach between Emperor and Pope over a whole range of ecclesiastical and political issues, culminating in the annexation of the Papal States by Napoleon (on the grounds that 'the Pope had constantly refused to make war on the English') and the arrest and deportation of the Pope and his exile from Rome from 1809 to 1814. It is ironic to recall one striking parallel with Henry VIII's quarrel with Rome – Napoleon's second marriage with Marie-Louise of Austria, after his previous barren union with the Empress Joséphine had been declared null by ecclesiastical courts in France without reference to the Holy See, and the refusal of 13 out of the 30 cardinals present in Paris to attend the ceremony.

From the Fall of Napoleon to the Separation of Church and State

The nineteenth century was a turbulent time for France politically, with the Consulate, the First Empire, the Bourbon Restoration, the July Monarchy (Louis-Philippe), the Second Republic, the Second Empire (Napoleon III), the Commune and the Third Republic following one after the other. It was a turbulent time for the Church as well. Three Archbishops of Paris were to meet violent deaths in the course of the century (Affre while trying to mediate on the barricades during the Revolution of 1848, Sibour stabbed during a church service in 1857 by a deranged priest whom he had suspended, Darboy executed by firing squad as a hostage of the *Commune* in 1871), while their predecessor, Mgr de Quelen, had to flee for his life in February 1831 as a violent Parisian mob destroyed the historic Archiepiscopal Palace, already badly damaged by rioters in the previous July. This is in marked contrast with the one recorded indignity suffered by an Archbishop of Canterbury during the same century – a dead cat flung into Howley's carriage during the demonstrations over the Reform Bill in 1832.

The life of the French Church during this period may be summarized under three headings.

Revival: The French Revolution had almost destroyed the Church; in spite of the Concordat it found itself at the time of the Bourbon Restoration in a very weak condition – spiritually and intellectually as well as materially. A number of eminent figures did much to restore its vitality, among them Dom Guéranger (1805-75), Abbot of Solesmes and restorer of Benedictine monasticism; Père Lacordaire (1802-61), champion of political Liberalism, restorer of the Dominican Order in France and an eloquent preacher whose sermons in Notre-Dame in Paris were perhaps as influential as those of Newman in St Mary's, Oxford; Cardinal Lavigerie (1825-92), Archbishop of Algiers and an outstanding missionary, the founder of the White Fathers and the Missionary Sisters of Africa and the implacable foe of slavery; and Frédéric Ozanam (1813-53), founder of the Society of St Vincent de Paul, an association of lay people committed to personal service among the poor. It is impossible to quantify the influence of the Saints in such a revival, but among the French saints of the nineteenth century are the Curé d'Ars (Jean-Marie Vianney – 1786-1859), Saint Bernadette, the visionary of Lourdes (1844-79), Saint Thérèse de Lisieux (1873-97) and (though as yet uncanonized) Charles de Foucauld (b. 1858), who was killed in 1916. The period was also one of intellectual (if not strictly theological) and literary revival under the aegis of such varied figures as Chateaubriand, Montalembert and Lamennais. The July Monarchy also saw the beginnings of the Social Gospel movement, which was to remain a strong tradition in French Catholicism.

Theological Controversy: This period was to see a titanic struggle between the Gallican and Ultramontane parties for control of the destinies of the French Church. Both 'Royal Gallicanism', with its loyalty to the House of Bourbon and to the old alliance of Altar and Throne, and 'Civil Gallicanism', with its attachment to the role of the State under whatever régime, were too deferential to the political and intellectual establishment and too much bound up with the defence of the privileges of the French Church. 'Episcopal Gallicanism', however, was a learned and principled defence of conciliarist ideas and of the rights of national churches and of individual bishops in the face of the papal

St Jean-Marie Vianney, Curé d'Ars, patron saint of the parish clergy

absolutism, liturgical uniformity and curial centralization championed by Pius IX. Among the most notable spokesmen before and during the First Vatican Council for the 'Inopportunists', who opposed the definition of the infallibility and universal jurisdiction of the Pope, were Darboy, Archbishop of Paris, and Dupanloup, Bishop of Orléans. Their failure to prevent the definition in 1870 represented the death knell of classical Gallicanism and the apparent triumph of the Ultramontanes. This latter party, though at first attracting a number of political liberals around the newspaper *L'Avenir* (with its motto 'God and Liberty') and its editor, the Abbé Lamennais (later to die condemned by, and unreconciled with, the Holy See), was ultra-papalist and very rigid in its theology; its chief French protagonists at the First Vatican Council were Cardinal Pie, Bishop of Poitiers, and the brilliant but lethal polemicist, Louis Veuillot (whose success was to anticipate that – in a very different cause – of the journalists, many of them French and Belgian, at the Second Vatican Council).

Church-State relations: It was understandable that at the Restoration most French Catholics would breathe a sigh of relief and welcome the return of the Bourbons, since for them the Revolution had appeared as the implacable foe and deadly persecutor of the Church. However, the Bourbon Restoration was not destined to last very long, and this was due in large measure to the blindly reactionary views of the ultra-Catholic

Charles X (1824-1830). Because of the close alliance of Altar and Throne, the Church was also to suffer from the 1830 revolution, which deposed the last King of France and put in his place 'the King of the French', Louis-Philippe (son of Philippe-Egalité, the regicide Duc d'Orléans). His liberal bourgeois régime was strongly tinged with anti-clericalism, leading to clashes with the Church over the state monopoly in education. It was only in 1833 that the Church won the right to have primary schools of its own and not until 1850 that it could have secondary education of its own. The year of philo-sophy – a prerequisite to the all-important *baccalauréat* – still had to be done in state schools, where the teaching then given seemed to the Church to be incompatible with its faith. So when in 1848 a further revolution forced Louis-Philippe to abdication and exile, most Catholics at first welcomed the short-lived Second Republic. Most of them likewise welcomed the 1851 *coup d'état* which led a year later to the Prince-President being proclaimed as the Emperor Napoleon III, for they were grateful to him for his military intervention in Italy to restore Pius IX's sovereignty over the Papal States.

It was the fall of Napoleon III in 1870 and the eventual establishment of the Third Republic that were to inaugurate a period of crisis in Church-State relations. In the confusion that followed the defeat and humiliation of 1870 and 1871, Catholics threw away their initially strong position by espousing the cause of the Monarchy (and the Bourbon claimant *might* have become King if he had not refused to accept the tricolour), by pressing for armed intervention in Italy to restore the Pope's temporal sovereignty and by other short-sighted and provocative policies. Their enemies made the most of Pius IX's disastrous *Syllabus of Errors* of 1864, which condemned *inter alia* the propo-sition that the Roman Pontiff should reconcile himself to 'progress, liberalism and modern civilization'. As one far-sighted priest, the Abbé Frémont, who unfortunately represented only a tiny minority of his colleagues, sadly commented,

> Because it has bound up its cause with that of Royalism, the clergy of France has finally convinced everyone who believes in things popular and democratic that between the Church on the one hand and progress, the Republic and the future on the other, there is no relationship possible but the most deadly hatred.[3]

The Republican counter-attack, which began in 1879, did not initially aim at total sepa-ration of Church and State, since the Concordat was seen as a useful and even necessary means for preserving some state control of the Church and preventing it from becoming totally subservient to Rome. The first phase of the attack was the battle over National Education and the establishment of the principle of *laïcité*,[4] that is to say, the removal from the syllabus of all religious teaching and its replacement by *civisme* – moral and civic instruction. This first phase was also to see the removal of religion from all state

---

3   Cf. J. McManners, *Church and State in France, 1870-1914* (London, 1972), p.44.

4   *Laïcité* was an unfortunate and confusing neologism which first made its appearance in the French language in the 1870s. It is necessary to distinguish between *laïcité, laïcisme* and the *école laïque* on the one hand (meaning secular, non- or even anti-religious) and *laïc/laïque* (layman/laywoman) and *laïcat* (the laity), as used within the Church, on the other hand.

ceremonies (no prayers in Parliament, the removal of the crucifix from schools and law courts, etc), the legalization of divorce and Sunday work, the suppression of army and hospital chaplaincies and the provision of secular funerals. It also involved an attack on the religious communities and their role in education; the Jesuits were inevitably a principal target. It is important to realize that throughout most of the nineteenth century there were no church-controlled institutions of higher education in theology in France. The faculties of theology planned for the state universities in the Napoleonic blueprint had – for a variety of reasons – never had more than a theoretical existence; they were finally suppressed in 1886. After 1875 it was possible for the Church to set up independent institutions of higher education with faculties of theology, but these soon had to call themselves *Instituts catholiques* as they were refused the status and title of universities and the right to confer degrees. To appreciate this situation and the bitter conflict which it caused, Anglicans need to imagine what the effect would have been on the Church of England if the universities of Oxford and Cambridge had been completely secularized and the Church had found itself without any institutions of higher education.

As the century drew to its close, there was, first of all, the glimmer of a hope of better relations when Pope Leo XIII advocated the policy of *ralliement* – loyal adherence to the established (i.e. republican) form of government. Things got worse, however, when the celebrated *Affaire Dreyfus* raised passionate feelings on both sides. Dreyfus was a Jewish army officer unjustly accused and imprisoned on charges of treason. Some Catholics supported him, but a larger number, openly anti-semitic, opposed him; the majority, by remaining silent and leaving the defence of justice to others, contributed to the growing strength of anticlericalism.

When it eventually came about, the Separation of Church and State proved to be a fierce and bitter rupture. All hope of compromise disappeared when, on the one side, Leo XIII was succeeded in 1903 by the saintly but narrow and inexperienced Pius X, who chose as his Secretary of State the intransigent Cardinal Merry del Val, and when, on the other side, the General Election of 1902 brought into power as Prime Minister the equally intransigent anticlerical (and rejected seminarian) Emile Combes.

The final separation was effected in three overlapping stages. The first concerned the religious orders. In 1901 the previous government had passed a Law on Associations, obliging all religious congregations to apply for state authorization. Some of the orders were obvious targets for even the more moderate anticlericals; the Assumptionists, who published the violently anti-Dreyfusard journal *La Croix*, had already been suppressed in 1900. However, the Combes government was determined to apply the legislation with the utmost rigour. All the women's orders were refused recognition, and this was also the case for all but five of the male orders. Notable among the exceptions were the *Pères Blancs* and the *Missions Africaines*; the government's anticlericalism was not for export, since the missionaries were seen by them as useful agents of their colonial policy. One of the principal aims of this legislation was of course to exclude entirely all members of religious congregations, male and female, from teaching in any schools or educational establishments in France. As Combes himself explained, 'Liberty of education is not one of those essential rights which are inseparable from the person of the citizen'.[5]

The second stage saw a series of incidents which concerned disputes over the role of the government in the nomination of bishops, attempts by Rome to remove two 'republican' bishops (one accused of having been seen wearing a masonic apron!) and a controversial state visit by the President of the French Republic to the King of Italy in Rome (which Merry del Val chose to condemn as a deliberate insult to the Pope). These led in July 1904 to the rupture of diplomatic relations between France and the Holy See, only resumed in a cautious and gradual process between 1921 and 1924.

The final stage of the rupture – the rejection of the Concordat and the total separation of the Church and State – followed with a kind of fatal inevitability in 1905, even though Combes was no longer Prime Minister when the Law of Separation was officially promulgated. The Law of Separation recognized freedom of conscience and guaranteed the free exercise of worship; it withdrew all financial support from religious organizations – except for some chaplaincies in public institutions; it declared all buildings used for worship or to lodge ministers of religion (including episcopal palaces and seminaries) to be the property of the State, the *département* or the commune (but with the proviso that churches should be available for worship without charge), and it arranged for the transfer of property, estates and legacies to legally recognized *associations cultuelles*. Catholics bitterly opposed the legislation, though some of the more far-sighted welcomed the independence of state control it would give to the Church. Two of its clauses caused particular controversy. One was the provision for inventories to be taken in churches, which led some officials to require the clergy to open their tabernacles for inspection; this provoked serious riots in many places. The other was the setting up of the *associations cultuelles*. Though this caused no problems for the Protestants or the Jews, Catholics saw this as a potential threat to episcopal and papal authority, with dissident clergy and lay people being encouraged to defy the hierarchy. In any case, Pius X soon rendered compromise impossible by an outright condemnation. An impasse resulted which was only gradually resolved in the better climate which prevailed after the First World War, when Catholics and anticlericals had been forged into a *union sacrée* against the invader, and when 25,000 priests and seminarians had been called up (of whom 5,000 lost their lives). The new climate was given symbolic recognition by the canonization of Joan of Arc in 1920, one of the last acts of a pope, Benedict XV, who had been bitterly and unfairly attacked in France (as pro-German and pro-Austrian) for his attempts to bring the war to an end and who was deeply saddened by the successful efforts of France and Italy to deprive the Holy See of any role in the peace negotiations and in the newly-founded League of Nations.

---

5   Cf. J. McManners, *op. cit.*, p.132.

Sur l'ordre du Préfet, les pompiers inondent l'église du Gros-Caillou.

The riots over the 'inventories'. Firemen are called out to disperse the faithful in a Parisian church.

From the Separation of the Church and State to the Second Vatican Council

The Church in France was – at least in the short term – terribly weakened by the long struggle over the separation of Church and State and its culmination in apparently total defeat and deprivation. The most obvious losses were financial (with the clergy reduced to real poverty), but there was also a significant decline in church attendance and a dramatic drop in the number of ordinations – from 1,753 in 1901 to 825 in 1913.

In spite of all this, the general picture of the French Church in the period up to the end of the Second Vatican Council is one of vitality, recovery and intellectual and spiritual strength. Added to all its other problems were two more, which were at the same time signs of its vitality. The first was the theological crisis over Modernism, involving men of the calibre of the church historian Louis Duchesne (1843-1922) and the scripture scholar Alfred Loisy (1857-1940) – both of whom taught at the *Institut Catholique de Paris* – in

13

The Concordat Alive and Well in Alsace-Lorraine

In speaking of Church-State relations in France it is necessary to make an exception of the two dioceses of Strasbourg and Metz. In 1870 Alsace-Lorraine was annexed by Germany, and it did not return to French sovereignty until 1918; it was not therefore affected by the anticlerical legislation which had so radically altered relations between Church and State in the rest of France. In these two dioceses the Napoleonic Concordat of 1801 (with some modifications, as far as religious education was concerned, brought in by the 1850 *Loi Falloux*) was still operating in 1918, and to this day it remains the basic foundation of Church-State relations there. The Concordat recognizes four *cultes*; the Lutheran Church, the Reformed Church and the Jews, as well as the Catholic Church. The principal ways in which it affects the Church are as follows:

–   There are notable financial advantages, which include the state remuneration of the clergy – those, at least, whose offices are recognized by the Concordat.

–   Religious instruction is given by authorized representatives of the four *cultes* in the state schools (though parents have the right to withdraw their children) and there are Catholic and Protestant faculties of theology at the University of Strasbourg which have the right to grant *diplômes d'Etat* in theology.

–   The State has a role in appointments to the more important ecclesiastical offices; more particularly, the Archbishop of Strasbourg and the Bishop of Metz are jointly appointed by the Holy See and the President of the Republic at the end of the normal process of consultation which applies to every diocese.

It is interesting to note that, when asked whether the Concordat makes it easier or more difficult for the Church in Alsace-Lorraine to fulfil its mission in society than for the Church in the rest of France, most Catholics there will reply that it makes no difference either way; it is seen neither as an advantage nor as an embarrassment. This is relevant to the debate in the Church of England over Establishment, since it suggests that a middle way is possible between being the Established Church and being an inward-looking sect. It is, moreover, certainly the case that the better financial remuneration of the clergy there has not exempted Alsace-Lorraine from the crisis of priestly vocations which affects the whole of France.

a doomed battle against Roman intransigence;[6] th' econd was the conflict between two rival visions of the role of Catholics in politics. The first of these two visions was that of the movement called *Le Sillon* (The Furrow) and of its dynamic leader, Marc Sangnier (1873-1950), precursor of Christian Democracy. *Le Sillon*, though inspired by Leo XIII's encyclical *Rerum Novarum* and his encouragement of the policy of *ralliement* to the Republic, was condemned by Pius X in 1910, but Sangnier himself, prudently submitting to the condemnation, lived on to encourage spiritual and social initiatives among French Catholics and to be the inspiration of the *Mouvement républicain populaire* (MRP), the Christian Democratic party which emerged from the Resistance to the Nazi occupation of the 1940s. The opposing vision was that of the *Action française* and of its formidable leader, Charles Maurras (1868-1952). Maurras was of the extreme right, a royalist and a nationalist who strove for the Church's blessing on his movement, although he did not become a believing and practising Catholic until after his imprisonment at the end of the Second World War as a supporter of the Vichy régime. The movement was at first favoured by Pius X, but he was preparing to condemn it when he died in 1914; it was formally condemned by Pius XI in 1926 and 1927, but the ban was in turn lifted by Pius XII in 1939. To understand the *intégriste* mentality of the French Catholic extreme right and the movement of rebellion against the Second Vatican Council led by Archbishop Marcel Lefebvre it is necessary to perceive the direct link between them and the *Action française*.

The twentieth century has also proved a phenomenal period for the contribution of Catholics (some of whom had notable conversion experiences) to the cultural, literary, philosophical and scientific life of France.[7] Among theologians there are also to be counted persons of the stature of Bouyer, Chenu, Congar, Daniélou, de Lubac and (in a rather different field) Teilhard de Chardin. Some of them were to experience being criticized and even condemned and disciplined under Pius XII and then being enlisted as *periti* (experts) or at least being quoted and praised at the Second Vatican Council; three of them (Daniélou, de Lubac and Congar) were to become cardinals.

The Third Republic, which at the beginning of the century had been so militantly anti-clerical but had established a reasonable *modus vivendi* with the Church by 1940, came to an end in that year under the German occupation. The Vichy régime of Marshal Pétain, which replaced it, represented, especially in its early phases, a real temptation to the Church, whose support it tried to win by important concessions, particularly in the field of education. In time, most of the Church's leaders began to distance themselves from the régime, especially when it began to embark on antisemitic legislation. Yet although Catholics, including many clergy and religious, took an often heroic part in the Resistance, the first Nuncio to the newly established Fourth Republic, Mgr Angelo Roncalli (the future Pope John XXIII), found on his desk after his arrival in Paris in

---

6   From another point of view the Roman battle against Modernism, though disastrously mistaken and notably unjust in so many of its particular judgements, can be seen as a necessary stand against efforts to subvert the very foundations of the Faith.

7   Any list would be arbitrary, but some of the most important names are surely those of Bernanos, Blondel, Claudel, Gilson, Maritain, Massignon, Mauriac, Mounier and Péguy among writers and thinkers, and Duruflé, Langlais, Messiaen, Poulenc and Rouault among artists and musicians.

The newly arrived Papal Nuncio, Mgr Roncalli, addresses General de Gaulle on behalf of the Diplomatic Corps on New Year's Day, 1945

December 1944 a dossier demanding the dismissal of forty bishops. These were judged by General de Gaulle and his Foreign Minister, Georges Bidault, both practising Catholics, to have compromised themselves seriously in the policy of 'collaboration'. It was no small tribute to Roncalli's diplomatic skill that the affair was resolved with the resignation of four bishops from mainland France and three more from overseas.[8]

The 1940s and '50s were a volatile period for the French Church, and Mgr Roncalli soon had an even more intractable problem to cope with. The drama of the Nazi occupation and of the forced labour camps in Germany had led many priests, who shared in the hardships of these experiences, to measure the real chasm that existed between the Church and the working class and at the same time to feel close to the workers through shared suffering and danger. This led to the search for more adventurous and more radical ways of expressing this new-found solidarity and building upon it. Among these were the foundation by Cardinal Suhard, Archbishop of Paris, of the *Mission de France* in 1941 and the *Mission de Paris* in 1943; both were formed to work exclusively in the de-christianized sectors of French society, which in the case of the latter meant among the urban proletariat. Books such as Godin's *France, Pays de Mission?* and Michonneau's *Paroisse Communauté Missionaire*,[9] soon translated into English, were to have a profound influence on the

---

[8]   Historians have not been able to get sight of Bidault's list; estimates therefore vary as to the number of names on it and the number of resignations obtained.

[9]   The English editions are M. Ward, *France Pagan?* (London, 1950) and E. Michonneau, *Revolution in a City Parish* (London, 1949).

16

post-war generation of Anglican clergy, particularly on Ted Wickham, leader of the Sheffield Industrial Mission, author of *Church and People in an Industrial City* (1957) and Bishop of Middleton from 1959 to 1982. In order to bridge the gap of hostility and incomprehension which separated the urban proletariat from the Church, an experiment was undertaken whereby 'worker priests' entered into full-time employment in factories and in manual labour. But this act of commitment to the working classes led – perhaps inevitably – to the involvement of many of these worker priests in the trades unions (and notably in the Communist CGT), in strike action and even, as members or sympathizers, in the powerful Communist Party. The bishops soon began to be seriously worried and Pius XII to feel that action was necessary. Roncalli, torn between his allegiance to Pius XII and his desire to understand and to interpret to Rome the motives which animated men like Cardinal Suhard, tried to prevent a condemnation. He was helped neither by the rigid anti-communism of the Roman curia nor by the intemperate language and political naïveté of some of the *prêtres-ouvriers*; in 1953 he became Cardinal Patriarch of Venice and in 1954 the blow fell. Pius XII forbad priests to be full-time workers and ordered those in full-time work to leave it by 1 March; more than half of them refused. A little later, however, he did authorize the re-opening at Pontigny of the Seminary of the *Mission de France*, and priests of the Mission were gradually allowed to engage in part-time manual labour as *prêtres au travail* (priests at work). Later still, Paul VI was to define more closely the status of priests of the *Mission de France*. Today it is organized as a Prelature under its own bishop. It has its headquarters at Pontigny in the Yonne and its seminary at Fontenay-sous-Bois outside Paris; twenty-seven of its 274 priests are working in countries of the third world.

Obedience to Rome was not an easy exercise in France at this time either for theologians or for worker priests. Among those who had tried to speak on their behalf were Roncalli (the future John XXIII) and Montini (the future Paul VI), though neither did so uncritically. As Jacques Maritain observed in 1948,

> France is light-years ahead of other countries. Hence the ambivalence of the Holy See in its regard; if the Holy See slams on the brakes, this is not because France is in error, but because France is way ahead. But one knows that it is opening the ways of the Lord, and that the rest of Christendom will follow where France has gone.[10]

When the Council came, it both released a long suppressed and potentially dangerous head of steam building up inside the Church in France and also opened the doors, as we shall see, to new problems and new crises.

---

[10] Quoted in the obituary of Cardinal Congar in the *Daily Telegraph* (14.7.95). It is from a 'swan-song speech' in Rome at the end of his time as French Ambassador to the Holy See, recorded by Peter Hebblethwaite, *Paul VI* (London, 1993), pp.216-7.

II THE CHURCH TODAY: BASIC INFORMATION

Membership

The population of France is over 57,000,000.[1] About 45,000,000 of these have been baptized as Catholics, and of these 10,000,000 can be considered as regular communicants (*pratiquants réguliers*) and another 10,000,000 as occasional communicants (*pratiquants occasionnels*). In 1954 those who were baptized as Catholics constituted 94% of the population, but between 1965 and 1985 regular Sunday mass attendance fell from 25% to 10% of the population. Among non-Catholic Christians the Protestant churches can number 850-900,000 adherents and the Orthodox churches 150-200,000. There are about 4,000,000 Muslims, nearly 600,000 Buddhists and 500-700,000 Jews.

The Episcopate

The French Episcopal Conference, which meets in plenary assembly every year in Lourdes, had in January 1995 115 members, in the following categories:

from Metropolitan France

17 Archbishops (including 3 Cardinals – Bordeaux, Marseille and Paris)
74 Diocesan Bishops
2 Coadjutor Bishops (with right of succession)
10 Auxiliary Bishops
1 Bishop for the Armed Forces
2 Bishops of Eastern Rite (Armenian and Ukrainian)
4 Diocesan Administrators (for vacant archiepiscopal and episcopal
sees and the prelacy of the *Mission de France*)

from Overseas (*départements d'outre-mer,* DOM)

1 Archbishop
3 Diocesan Bishops
1 Vicar Apostolic

The Statutes and Standing Orders of the Conference, approved by the Holy See, are designed to enable the French bishops to exercise a collegial responsibility for the mission and pastoral service of the Church at the national level, while carefully respecting the authority of each bishop within his own diocese. The Conference elects its own President; currently (in 1995) this office is held by the Archbishop of Rouen, Mgr Joseph Duval, who succeeded Cardinal Decourtray of Lyon in 1990, who in turn succeeded Bishop Vilnet of Lille, himself neither a Cardinal nor an Archbishop. There is in fact no *ex officio* Primate of the French Church, although the Archbishop of Paris

---

[1] Most of the figures in this chapter are taken from the 1995 edition of *L'Église Catholique en France*, the year book of the French Episcopal Conference.

is the only bishop who in virtue of his see is a permanent member of the Standing Committee of the Conference, a body which meets every month. The Conference also has a Secretariat General (with a Secretary General – a priest – elected by the Assembly), four Assistant General Secretaries and a number of national bodies depending upon it: the Doctrinal Commission (whose influential secretary is Mgr Damien Sicard), ten other Episcopal Commissions (including the Commission for Christian Unity), four Episcopal Committees and a number of other national organizations.

At the regional level there are nine 'apostolic regions', which have effectively replaced the former ecclesiastical provinces, so that today – except for the more important sees such as Paris and Lyon – the distinction between archbishops and bishops is almost solely historical. In each of these new regions the bishops elect one of their number as chairman for a term of years. Thus, for example, the current Chairman of the Apostolic Region of the Midi is the Bishop of Cahors, although his region includes the archbishoprics of Albi, Auch and Toulouse.[2] All of these apostolic regions are represented on the Standing Committee of the Episcopal Conference and on each of the Episcopal Commissions.

Diocesan Synods

The new Code of Canon Law of 1983 has given renewed vitality to an ancient institution by opening full participation in a diocesan synod to the laity. A diocesan synod according to the new Code is not, as in the Church of England, a permanent body meeting two or three times every year; it is convoked by its bishop for a session which may last from two to four years and which at the end of its work may resolve to hold another after an interval of five years or so. It does, however, try to mobilize the participation of all the faithful in one way or another, for it is normally preceded by a vast consultation which may involve evaluating several thousand replies (from individuals or from groups) to questionnaires sent out beforehand. Each diocese is free to decide both as to whether and when to hold a synod and also on what basis to organize the election of those of its members who are not members *ex officio*. A synod is seen as a spiritual pilgrimage (since the word 'synod' comes from a Greek verb meaning to walk together) and as an adventure in and a commitment to Christian mission; it is concerned to arrive at and to articulate a consensus on the questions put before it. It is not, however, just a debating chamber, since it can and does vote propositions which can become part of diocesan law. The bishop alone convokes the synod and signs its declarations and decrees, which are published under his authority, but he can only promulgate as synodical laws propositions made by the synod and in the form in which the synod has passed them to him. He has nonetheless the obligation to ensure that none of these propositions is likely to endanger the communion his diocese has to maintain with other local churches and with the See of Rome. So, for example, a certain number of questions discussed in diocesan synods have been judged to exceed the competence of a local or

---

2   For a map of the dioceses and apostolic regions of Metropolitan France, see p.vi.

Cahors: Portrait of a Rural Diocese in the Midi – 'la France profonde'

Area: The *Département* of the Lot; 5,216.53 square kilometres (1% of the territory of metropolitan France); population 155,000. A predominantly rural and agricultural area, attracting large numbers of tourists – especially from Great Britain, and with 497 registered British nationals in 1990. The seat of the Prefecture and of the Bishop is the ancient city of Cahors, with a population of about 20,000, famous for its great mediaeval bridge and for its wine. In the thirteenth century it was one of the great cities of France; its decline was due in large measure to the Hundred Years' War. Among its more illustrious children were an Avignon pope, John XXII, and a leading nineteenth-century anticlerical, Léon Gambetta.

The Church: The present Bishop is Mgr Maurice Gaidon, born in 1928 and appointed to the see in 1987. He is a member of the Episcopal Commission for Clergy and Seminaries and while at Paray-le-Monial (Diocese of Autun) helped to develop that famous pilgrimage centre as the focus for charismatic renewal and the 'New Communities' and as the site of a new seminary. Cahors is part of the Apostolic Region of the Midi (formerly it was in the Province of Albi) and its Bishop is currently President of the Region. The boundaries of the diocese were changed by the Napoleonic Concordat (and, indeed, earlier for the Constitutional Church) and the diocese of Montauban was created to correspond with the *Département* of the Lot-et-Garonne. There are 126 priests in the diocese, of whom 21 are retired and 82 in full-time ministry; 104 of them are 60 or over. There are two permanent deacons (and one soon to be ordained), three congregations of male religious (none contemplative or monastic) and about 200 sisters (two houses of contemplatives and ten congregations of active religions). In six years Mgr Gaidon has ordained five priests (in the previous eleven years there were no ordinations) and he has at present nine seminarians in training. There are 403 parishes; of the population about 80% are baptized Catholics, 10 to 12% are regularly at Sunday Mass, 40 to 50% of children of twelve and under follow the Catechism (in some parishes almost all the children). Three laywomen are *'permanentes en pastorale'* in full-time diocesan ministry.

A place of pilgrimage: The shrine of Our Lady (*La Vierge Noire*) of Rocamadour is (with Chartres and Le Puy) one of the most ancient Marian sanctuaries of France. Among early pilgrims were Henry II of England, St Louis (Louis IX) of France, St Bernard and St Dominic. A more modern pilgrim was the composer Francis Poulenc, whose *Litanies à la Vierge Noire* are well known and who attributed his conversion to Our Lady of Rocamadour. The site, with chapels and fortresses built into the steep cliffs, attracts vast numbers of tourists and pilgrims. Mgr Gaidon plans to develop Rocamadour not only as a place of pilgrimage but as a centre of renewal and inspiration for the whole diocese.

*The shrine of Our Lady of Rocamadour and (inset) Mgr Gaidon,
Bishop of Cahors*

particular church; nevertheless, some of their recommendations on such subjects – such
as those of the Synod of Lyon on the ordination of married men to the priesthood and
the admission of the divorced and remarried to the sacraments – have been transmitted
to Rome.

A number of French dioceses not yet ready for a full synod have engaged or are engag-
ing in various kinds of pre-synod projects. Thirty-four diocesan synods have been
completed and there were still three at work at the beginning of 1995.

Theological Pluralism

Gallicanism, in the strict sense of a doctrinal system which affirmed the superiority of General Councils over the Pope and the quasi autonomy of a national church, is certainly dead. However, a certain Gallican spirit, based on a real and deep fidelity to the See of Rome that is neither uncritical nor subservient, is still very much alive. The Church in France is less obviously marked, at least at the level of its episcopate, by extreme polarization between conservative and radical tendencies than the Church in some other countries of Western Europe; indeed, one has the impression that today theological pluralism is more of a reality than it perhaps was twenty years ago. Then, most of the bishops came from a background of involvement in the different sectors of Catholic Action (see p.42 below), and would have laid stress on their *ouverture* (openness) to new ideas in the theological, pastoral and social domains. Today, they come from more diverse backgrounds. They include theologians of distinction such as Pierre Eyt, Archbishop of Bordeaux, recently created Cardinal and a former Rector of the *Instituts Catholiques* of Toulouse and Paris, and Claude Dagens, Bishop of Angoulême and a former Dean of the Faculty of Theology at Toulouse. A more conservative stance in theology, notable in some more recent episcopal appointments, must not be taken to suggest conservative views on social and political questions; the bishops have not hesitated to criticize the French government on a number of issues, such as that of the treatment of immigrants.

The most 'nonconformist' of the French bishops is without doubt Mgr Jacques Gaillot, Bishop of Evreux (Normandy) from 1982 to 1995. He is a man who is certainly not afraid of controversy and may even, through his readiness to exploit the media, be said to seek it. This led to his being disowned and rebuked on several occasions by his colleagues, and eventually to his dismissal.[3] Yet his 'nonconformity' is not so much to be sought in the strictly doctrinal field as in the domains of ethics, of ecclesiastical discipline and of socio-political questions. Behind his apparent readiness to shock and to challenge is a passionate concern to communicate the Gospel among those sections of the population who are most estranged from the Church. In marked contrast is the figure of Cardinal Jean-Marie Lustiger, Archbishop of Paris, but it would be wrong to think of him as an old-fashioned conservative; indeed, as a Jew who still affirms his Jewishness, he has attracted the odium of the anti-semitic right. He is close to Pope John Paul II and has no nostalgia for the pre-conciliar Church. He and his followers would prefer to be considered as *'catholiques classiques'* rather than as *'catholiques traditionalistes'*. A very substantial number of French bishops, particularly among the more recent appointments, will generally be found to vote with him at meetings of the Episcopal Conference, but – as one of them has said – this does not mean that they agree with everything he says or with his manner of saying it. He rules over his diocese with vigour and celebrates and preaches in his cathedral before a large congregation nearly every Sunday evening.

---

[3] See pp.43-4 below.

22

Cardinal Lustiger (front row, second from left) at a meeting of the French Episcopal Conference at Lourdes

Some of the leading exponents of change at the Second Vatican Council were French, but so was the bishop who led the traditionalist resistance to the Council, Archbishop Marcel Lefebvre. Formerly Archbishop of Dakar and Bishop of Tulle, it was as Superior General of the Congregation of the Holy Spirit (*Spiritains*) that he attended the Council. From one so deeply influenced by the *Action française* of Charles Maurras this opposition was not surprising. As he revealingly expressed it himself, he could only see in the Council the conquest of the Catholic Church by the spirit and principles of the French Revolution; the Decree on Religious Freedom was the equivalent of *Liberté*, the collegiality of bishops, as found in the Constitution of the Church, the equivalent of *Egalité*, the Decree on Ecumenism the equivalent of *Fraternité*. Mgr Lefebvre's movement was clearly a dissident one from the beginning and involved a number of acts of defiance, of which the most spectacular was the seizure, in a commando-style operation, of the Church of St-Nicolas-du-Chardonnet in Paris in 1977. This church remains in the hands of the Lefebvrists to this day, since both the civil and ecclesiastical authorities are reluctant to call in the police to repossess it by force. In 1988 a movement of rebellion was turned into the formal rupture of schism when Mgr Lefebvre, three years before his death, ordained illicitly four bishops at the seminary he had founded at Ecône in Switzerland and was promptly excommunicated together with the four bishops. This led to a division within the movement he founded; some followed him into schism but others made their peace with Rome, including a number of religious communities such as the Benedictine Abbey of Le Barroux in the Diocese of Avignon. Those priests who left Lefebvre's *Fraternité St-Pie X* were regrouped by Rome into a new *Fraternité St-*

Pierre and have been found a place – such as in the parish of Sainte-Odile in the seventeenth arrondissement of Paris – where they are authorized to celebrate according to the Mass of Pius V but as part of a team with priests who themselves use the new rite.[4]

Two moments in the political history of France in the last fifty or so years have contributed to the present pluralism in French Catholicism. The first was that of the Vichy Régime from 1940-44. The fact that a considerable number of the bishops preached the duty of loyalty to Marshal Pétain throughout that period led to a breach between the bishops and many of their clergy and people that bred a certain habit of disobedience among the latter and strengthened the move away from the association of the French Church with political conservatism. As one authoritative commentator has put it,

> This past has been neither forgotten nor totally amnestied. Graver still, the credibility of the magisterium has suffered lasting harm because of it... If we ask today about the origins of the crisis of the Church, it has to be agreed that the first crack dates from these years.[5]

The second moment was that of the *événements* (events) of May 1968, the heady days of student revolt which gave a powerful boost to the anti-authoritarian streak in the French temperament and certainly did not leave French Catholics unaffected. However, as we shall see, the anarchic libertarianism and permissiveness of May 1968 led to a reaction; some of the leaders of the movements of charismatic renewal in the French Church came from the ranks of disillusioned leaders of the student revolt. Such, for example, is Frère Ephraïm, a non-violent anarchist in 1968 and founder in 1973 of the community now known as the *Communauté des Béatitudes*.

The Church and Politics

The pluralism that is so evident a reality in the Church in France at the theological level is equally evident at the political level. Someone with extreme right-wing theological views is almost certain to have equally extreme right-wing political views, supporting both the ideas of Archbishop Lefebvre and the political programme of Le Pen's *Front national*. At the other end of the spectrum, a former Bishop of Orléans, Mgr Riobé, the *enfant terrible* of the French episcopate before Mgr Gaillot, would be found publicly opposing French possession of nuclear weapons in 1969 and advocating the ordination of married men to the priesthood in 1970. In the 1950s Jesuit and Dominican theologians had been censured by Rome both for their 'advanced' theology and for their support for the worker priests and for their political engagement. It is clear today that there is no longer any one party that can claim to be the Catholic or Christian Democrat

---

4   The *Fraternité St-Pierre* seems to be proving something of a transitional haven; some have now left it to be incardinated in the diocese in which they are working.

5   René Rémond (Président de la Fondation Nationale des Sciences Politiques) in *Etudes* (the monthly journal of the French Jesuits), September 1992.

party, although it looked in the years immediately following the Liberation as if the MRP (*Mouvement républicain populaire*), led by Georges Bidault and including Robert Schuman, 'the Father of Europe', architect-in-chief of Franco-German reconciliation and of the European Union, might fulfil that role. When it ceased to exist in 1967, its supporters having gradually been drawn away either to *Gaullisme* or to the Left, it had fulfilled an important role in establishing among French Catholics that sense of the necessity of a political pluralism within the limits of an acceptance of the Republic which was one of the seeds of its own demise. The restructuring of the Socialist Party by François Mitterand involved a deliberate desire to free French socialism from its historic anticlericalism and – despite setbacks occasioned by the ability of the sensitive issue of education to rekindle the dying embers of old quarrels – this has had a measure of success, demonstrated by the fact that one of its leading figures, Jacques Delors, is a convinced and practising Catholic. In the 1965 presidential elections 31% of occasionally practising Catholics and 25% of the regularly practising voted for Mitterand. A potent symbol of this new climate was the funeral mass, televised from Nevers Cathedral in 1993, of the former Socialist prime minister, Pierre Bérégovoy, after his tragic suicide, which was attended by almost all the French political 'establishment'.

In France the trades unions have traditionally been divided into three ideological groups: the Communist CGT, the Socialist FO and the Catholic CFTC (*Confédération française des travailleurs chrétiens* – French Confederation of Christian Workers). In 1964 this last movement 'de-confessionalized' itself, when the majority of its members formed the CFDT (*Confédération française démocratique du travail* – French Democratic Confederation of Labour). Though this new body has not denied its Christian roots and inspiration, it is now clearly and openly pluralist.[6]

In 1972, in the light of political evolution in France and of *Gaudium et Spes*, the Pastoral Constitution of Vatican II on the Church and the Modern World, the French Episcopal Conference issued (with 110 votes out of 112 in favour) an important and historic document, *Politique, Eglise et Foi: Pour une pratique chrétienne de la politique* (Politics, Church and Faith: Towards a Christian political practice). This clearly recognized not only the reality but the full legitimacy of political pluralism – of different political options – provided that they avoid totalitarianism or the denial of basic human rights; it also encouraged Christians to participate in the political life of their country. In the light of this document Catholics are called upon to engage in politics but no longer for a particular kind of politics.

The Church in France abstains from all political favouritism and yet feels free to make its voice heard on political and social issues which have a moral dimension. There is total separation of Church and State, but the Church, far from feeling marginalized, is able to intervene – whether to counsel and encourage politicians or to protest and remonstrate – in the consciousness that such intervention is less easily open to the accusation of self-interest than was once the case and more likely to be seen as the

---

[6] The old CFTC still continues, since a minority of its members refused to accept the change.

expression of the conscientious conviction of a not inconsiderable percentage of the French population.

Education

Except in Alsace-Lorraine, state education in France is entirely 'neutral'; no religious teaching of any kind may figure in its syllabus.[7] However, 83% of children in primary and secondary education are being taught in the public sector, and parents who desire Catholic teaching for their children have the right to ask for it. For children in primary schools it is the responsibility of the parish – the *curé* and his team of lay teachers – to organize catechetical instruction; this happens at present on Wednesdays – a mid-week free day made available by the State – and not on Sundays. For the state secondary schools – *collegès* (junior secondary) and *lycées* (upper secondary) – parents have the right to ask for the creation of a chaplaincy (*aumonêrie d'enseignement public* – AEP) which operates alongside the school. At the last count there were 3,200 such chaplaincies for a total of 7,851 establishments, and in 1992 they were dealing with 240,000 children. With the drop in the number of priests and religious there has been the rise of *permanents laïcs* – lay men and women (some of them full-time and salaried), properly trained and formally accredited by the Church – in charge of an increasing number of AEPs. The principle of the free Wednesday – under fire now even at the level of the primary schools – no longer applies universally to the secondary schools; at this level, because it implies a full teaching morning on Saturday and is therefore under threat from those who would like *'le weekend anglais'*, it is even more fragile. The chaplaincies, however, are open in the evenings and at weekends for a wide variety of activities; whether they are allowed to use buildings on the school premises or have to operate from outside is a question for the head and the governing body to decide.

Catholic schools also exist and are stronger in some parts of the country (e.g. in the regions of Rennes and Nantes) than in others; nearly 95% of pupils in the private sector are in Catholic schools. Practically all of these are *sous contrat* (under contract), following the state education system and agreeing to meet its requirements, and therefore receive financial support from the government in the form of staff salaries and part of their running costs. Mixed motives prevail among parents in France as in England in the choice of schools for their children; good Catholic parents may conscientiously opt for the state system for their children, while Church schools may be favoured by non-practising Catholic or non-Catholic parents for a variety of reasons; strict Muslims, for example, will choose single-sex schools (even convent schools) for their daughters.

One of the bitterest battlefields in the story of the separation of Church and State was that of education, and the battle cry of the *école laïque*[8] is still resurrected from time to time. The main teachers' union, the *Fédération de l'Education Nationale*, still keeps

---

7   For the situation in Alsace-Lorraine, see p.14 above.

8   Cf. pp.10-12 above.

alive the old anticlerical tradition and is firmly opposed to state aid for church schools. Most of the historic bitterness disappeared after the Second World War; today's Socialist Party, as already noted, contains many practising Catholics anxious to free it from the stigma of anticlericalism. However, it would seem that the wounds of these old divisions have not been completely healed. In 1984 a vast crowd took to the streets in Paris to demonstrate in favour of Catholic schools – *L'école libre* – considered to be under threat from the government of the time, though many who demonstrated then were moved less by a strong attachment to Catholic education as such than by a belief in pluralism in education and in the virtue of a healthy competition between two systems. In January 1994 another vast crowd took to the streets in Paris to demonstrate in favour of the principle of *laïcité*, considered to be compromised by proposals to increase state aid to the *école libre*.

The same 'neutrality' or *laïcité* marks the state universities and the more prestigious *Grandes Ecoles*; there again the Church is free to organize chaplaincies to but not of these establishments. There are a number of Catholic universities or *Instituts Catholiques* (Angers, Lille, Lyon, Paris, Toulouse) and these – alongside some Protestant and Orthodox institutes – are the only places outside Alsace-Lorraine which provide faculties of theology.

A group of students outside the Institut Catholique de Paris

The Church's Finances

As we have seen in Chapter I, the separation of Church and State at the beginning of the century plunged the Church into a financial crisis and imposed great hardship on the clergy in particular. Now, at the end of the century, most French Catholics welcome with relief the fact that the vast majority of churches and presbyteries are the property of the State (e.g. the Cathedrals) or of the Commune, who not only own them but are responsible for their maintenance. The exception concerns those built or acquired since the Separation.

The basic economic unit of the French Church is the diocese. In each diocese there is a Diocesan Association (created in 1923) and the bishop organizes the finances of his diocese with his Diocesan Council for Economic Affairs (many of whose members are lay people). A separate régime of course prevails in the dioceses of Metz and Strasbourg where the Concordat is still in force.

Each diocese is called upon to contribute to the running of the Episcopal Conference and its national services and also to the Holy See – the *Denier de St-Pierre* or Peter's Pence. Within each diocese the first charge upon its finances is the remuneration of its clergy and (increasingly) of its full time lay *animateurs pastoraux*. The 1995 Year Book states that 'one can say that with very few exceptions priests receive a total monthly remuneration which, with certain benefits in kind in addition, averages F4,000 net'.[9] The method of remuneration varies from diocese to diocese; in some, but not in all, offerings made for masses and for other sacramental rites are centralized to ensure an equality of stipend for all the clergy. The main expense of each diocese after the remuneration of the clergy and their social security (compulsory for all ministers of religion and members of religious orders since 1978) is the construction and upkeep of a certain number of buildings, not only churches and presbyteries constructed since the Separation (of which there are many in the towns and new suburbs) but a considerable number of halls and meeting rooms.

Giving comes in a number of ways. First of all, the faithful are urged as a matter of duty to contribute to the *Denier de l'Eglise* or *Denier du Culte*; how much they give, how often and by what means, is left to their discretion, but it is nevertheless a form of planned giving. Secondly, there are collections taken at services either for the ordinary expenses of the Church or for particular causes such as the *Comité catholique contre la Faim et pour le Développement* (against hunger and for development). Thirdly, there are offerings made at baptisms, weddings, funerals and for mass intentions – often by those who are not regular worshippers. Fourthly, there are legacies or other kinds of financial gifts made directly to the diocese. The State allows tax relief on legacies and on the *Denier de l'Eglise*; it of course remunerates directly certain chaplains (Catholic, Protestant and Jewish) in the prisons, the armed services, etc.

---

9   *L'Église Catholique en France*, p.278.

The Ecumenical Scene

The final chapter is given over entirely to the question of relations between Anglicans and French Roman Catholics; nobody, however, could imagine for a moment that these form anything but a minor part in the total picture of French Catholic involvement in ecumenical dialogue and ecumenical relations.

Historically, Protestantism in France has two main sources; the principal one in the Reformed tradition, shaped decisively by the French Reformer, Jean Calvin, and the secondary one in the Lutheran tradition, emanating from those parts of Eastern France – notably Alsace – which were outside the Kingdom of France in the 16th century. Lutheranism is still strongest in the eastern provinces, but many Alsatians left their homeland when it was annexed by Germany in 1871 after the Franco-Prussian War and moved to other parts of France, to Paris in particular. There are also a number of other Protestant churches – some, like the Baptists, are members with the Reformed and Lutheran churches of the *Fédération Protestante de France*; others of a fundamentalist and anti-ecumenical character are not. To say that the history of Catholic-Protestant relations in France has not been a happy one would be a monumental understatement. There is still alive the memory of the Religious Wars of the sixteenth century, when it seemed for a time that there was a real possibility that France would become a Protestant country, and of the Massacre of St Bartholomew (1572) in particular; of the Revocation of the Edict of Nantes by Louis XIV and of the subsequent bitter persecution of the Protestants, many of whom found refuge in Britain, Germany, the Netherlands, North America and South Africa. Catholics, on the other hand, remember that many Protestants sided with the anticlericals in the struggles surrounding the Separation of Church and State and the *'laïcisation'* of education.

The situation began to change for the better – but only very gradually – during the course of the present century. Some of the great 'precursors' of Ecumenism among French Catholics only really entered into dialogue with French Protestants after they had been engaged for some time in dialogue with Anglicans and with the Eastern churches. With regard to the latter, it must be remembered that between the Russian Revolution and the Second World War, Paris became the capital of the Russian 'diaspora', with its theological and intellectual headquarters at the *Institut St-Serge* in the nineteenth arrondissement.[10] A determinative influence in changing the ecumenical climate (not only in France) was the Abbé Paul Couturier of Lyon, who between the two World Wars refounded the Week of Prayer for Christian Unity on a basis which allowed all Christians to participate without comprising their theological convictions. He also founded the *Groupe des Dombes* – an annual meeting of priests and pastors, normally held at the Trappist Abbaye des Dombes, to engage in theological dialogue in a climate of prayer and personal friendship. This group, though unofficial, has published a number of agreed statements which have had wide and deep repercussions well beyond

---

[10] There are now renewed links of a very positive nature between French Catholics and the Orthodox Churches of Eastern Europe, especially in Romania and Russia.

France. The process was helped by Catholic and Protestant co-operation in the Resistance to Nazism and by a post-Christian culture in France today which makes even more pressing the need for Christians to work together.

Today the French Church has an Episcopal Commission for Christian Unity with a national secretariat, a network of regional and diocesan delegates, and committees for dialogue with Reformed and Lutheran Protestants, with the Orthodox, with Anglicans and with Baptists. Significant advances have been made in France with regard to the dispositions for eucharistic hospitality (both for *foyers mixtes* – inter-church marriages – and ecumenical groups). There is also an increasing rapprochement both in the field of prayer and community life (with a notable lead being taken by the interconfessional community of Taizé) and in common witness and action in society.

The Abbé Paul Couturier, Apostle of Prayer for Christian Unity

Ecumenical co-operation has not only secured a common version of the Lord's Prayer but also a common translation of the Bible with notes and commentary, the TOB or *traduction oecuménique de la Bible*. This is currently being followed up by an attempt to produce an agreed translation of the Creeds. In 1987 a new institution came into existence, the *Conseil d'Eglises Chrétiennes en France* (Council of Christian Churches in France), which seeks to enable the different Christian confessions to make a common stand on certain issues which arise at a national level and to promote a deeper level of communion between the member churches.[11]

---

[11]   To this day Paris and Lyon remain the twin capitals of French Catholic ecumenical activity. In Paris can be found the headquarters of the national Secretariat for Christian Unity under Fr Guy Lourmande and in close conjunction with it the *Association pour l'Unité des Chrétiens* and its review *Unité des Chrétiens*, founded in 1970 by Canon Jacques Desseaux, the national Secretary at the time. In Lyon can be found the *Association Unité Chrétienne*, its review *Unité Chrétienne* and the Chair of Ecumenism at the Catholic University; all these were until recently under the direction of Fr Michalon, the Abbé Couturier's successor. Similarly, the work of the Dominican centre *Istina* in Paris, directed by Fr Bernard Dupuy, is complemented by the same Order's *Centre St-Irénée* in Lyon, directed by Fr René Beaupère.

III A CHURCH IN TRAVAIL:
POINTS OF CRISIS AND SIGNS OF HOPE

If it is no exaggeration to say that the Church in France today is a church in crisis, it is certainly necessary to attempt to locate that crisis more precisely. All the churches (of all denominations) in Western Europe (and beyond) are experiencing a crisis ('the crisis of Christendom') through the increasing secularization and dechristianization of the countries of a traditionally Christian culture in which they are set. This had begun earlier in France than in many of its neighbours; in England, for example, we have no experience of the striking and often extreme regional variations which in France date back to the French Revolution and to the bitter politico-religious divisions that accompanied and followed it. In France there are whole *départements* in which the percentage of practising Catholics ever since that time has been extremely small and others in which it has been very high – the latter category including not only rural areas like Brittany and the Vendée but some industrial areas near the Belgian frontier. The contrast is less extreme at the present time; this is due both to the increasing mobility of the population and to a serious drop in religious practice in traditionally Catholic areas.[1]

The Crisis of the Priesthood

The point at which the crisis in French Catholicism is felt most acutely is in the sharp drop in the number of the clergy, particularly among diocesan or 'secular' priests. One factor has been the number of those already ordained leaving the priesthood. Sometimes this has been in order to marry, but a more general malaise has been the crisis of identity of the priesthood – the feeling among many priests that their traditional sphere of work reduced them to being mere functionaries of '*le culte*', imprisoned by the increasingly irrelevant structures of an institution unable (or unwilling) to adapt to new situations, and that there were greater opportunities for a more direct and effective Christian witness available to the laity. Many were unable to cope with the changes introduced by the Council (and perhaps operated too rapidly in France) or with the challenges presented by the *événements* of May 1968; it was in the late '60s and in the 1970s that such departures from priestly ministry were at their height.

The other factor has been the alarming drop in the number of ordinations. The drop has in no way been confined to the last 20 years. In 1951 there were 991 ordinations, in 1961 575 and in 1972 only 216. In ten years, between 1965 and 1975, the number of diocesan priests fell from 40,900 to 36,000; in 1991 there were 24,624 (with another 6,940 priests in religious orders). In 1975 170 diocesan priests were ordained, in 1977 only 99. During the next ten years the annual figures fluctuated between 125 (1979) and 94 (1986). From 1988 the numbers increased to between 140 (1989) and 130 (1991), and since 1992 they

---

[1] Paradoxically, France has been called both *'la fille aînée de l'Eglise'* and *'le plus vieux pays laïc de la terre'* – both 'the eldest daughter of the Church' and 'the oldest secular nation on earth'.

'Because the world needs love, the Church needs you.' A reminder of the pressing need for more priests – a poster to be seen in many French churches

have stabilized at around 125. These figures relate only to the secular (diocesan) priest-hood. In 1993, for example, a further 38 religious were ordained to the priesthood.

Although in one sense the situation is improving (in that the sharpness of the fall in the number of ordinations is being arrested), in another sense it is getting worse. There is a missing generation in many dioceses between the large group of elderly priests and the small number of those recently ordained. Moreover, the number of the older generation is being steadily diminished by death and by retirement. The official retirement age is 75, and the fact that in very many dioceses the average age of the active clergy is over 65 points to a striking contrast to the Church of England, in which retirement is taken between 65 and 70.

The crisis has, of course, had inevitable consequences for the seminaries. Previously, every diocese had its own seminary. Indeed, each diocese had not only a major seminary (*grand séminaire*) but also a minor seminary (*petit séminaire*); these latter are now a phenomenon of the past. In addition, there were a number of *séminaires universitaires*, such as the *Séminaire des Carmes* at the *Institut Catholique de Paris*, and the *Séminaire pontifical français* at Rome. Now, although these latter have been maintained, seminaries mostly operate on a regional rather than a diocesan footing. Very often the two-year 'first cycle' for younger candidates takes place in one centre, followed by a break or *stage* (for the still compulsory military service or its equivalent). The 'second cycle' of four years (with part of the last two years being spent in a parish) follows in another centre. So, for example, for one region the first cycle is spent in Poitiers and the second in Bordeaux.

In a period which, on the whole, has been one of decline there have been some signs pointing in the opposite direction. In the selection of new bishops Rome has given prior-ity to those considered capable of reversing the trend and working energetically to foster vocations to the priesthood. One or two of these have even re-opened diocesan semi-naries (at Ars and at Toulon, for example) while Paray-le-Monial in the Diocese of Autun has become a lively centre not only of charismatic renewal but of preliminary training for the priesthood. It is indeed from the ranks of the 'new communities' inspired by the Charismatic Renewal (see pp.39-40 below) that a significant number of vocations to the priesthood are emerging. A particularly interesting experiment is being conducted in Paris, where Cardinal Lustiger has been working hard and with a considerable measure of success to encourage priestly vocations. In 1985 he established the *Séminaire de Paris* as a seminary without walls. This consists of one house which specializes in pre-seminary spiritual formation or *propédeutique* and a number of other houses (for first and second cycle seminarians) which are in fact large clergy houses attached to some of the parish churches in the centre of Paris, where the students live in small groups or *équipes* with one priest of the seminary staff living with them. One of these parish churches is St Roch, between the Opéra and the Tuileries, where the Superior, the Abbé Eric Aumonier, resides. It is interesting to note that a number of the seminarians come from the *Communauté de l'Emmanuel* and are well integrated into the life of the *équipe* of which they form part. Their *Studium* (programme of studies) is an integral part of another of the Cardinal's imaginative creations, the *Ecole Cathédrale* (Cathedral School), which offers to the laity courses in Scripture, Doctrine, Moral Theology, Patristics, Spirituality, Philosophy, Liturgy, Pastoralia and Sacred Art. The teaching given in the *Studium*, however, is not normally open to the public.

Other new initiatives have included the creation of a certain number of communities, allowing secular priests to live together with a degree of common life. A striking example is the *Communauté St-Martin*, which now has its own seminary at Candé-sur-Beuvron in the Diocese of Blois. At first this community was not welcomed by the French bishops, and it was given a home by the very conservative Cardinal Siri at Genoa. It has, however, now been operating for a number of years in France; it was first invited into a French diocese by the Bishop of Fréjus and Toulon. Many English holiday-makers in the Var have been impressed by this young and dynamic community, by their dignified liturgy (traditional in feel but not at all Lefebvrist) and their thoughtful preaching, their ecumenical openness and the restoration of seemliness to the churches in their care. Four or five priests live together in a presbytery and look after half a dozen or more villages in the surrounding area; this is a pattern which is sure to attract imitation far beyond the membership of this particular community.

When it comes to trying to draw some conclusions from this situation, it would seem that two sharply contrasted analyses of the crisis of vocations to the secular priesthood in the French Church are competing for endorsement. The only point which they have in common is that they both locate the heart of the matter in the controversy over the *identity* of the priest.

The first analysis lays the responsibility upon the refusal of those in authority to abandon – or even to modify – the traditional (i.e. mediaeval and post-Tridentine) image of the secular priest. This criticism is directed in the first place at the continuing obligation of celibacy, but sees this in the context of a whole set of structures and attitudes which are part of the same lifestyle 'package'. Those in this camp – including a great number of older priests – have given up trying to encourage vocations; they are motivated not only by discouragement and despair but also, in many cases, by the conviction that the secular priesthood *as it now exists* has to wither away so that those in authority (especially in Rome) will be forced to accept a radical change of policy. A large number of older priests are quite simply overworked and exhausted, with their time almost exclusively taken up by providing the sacraments; their loyalty to the Church and their willingness to carry on in full-time ministry until the age of 75 do not prevent many of them from giving firm and formal notice to their bishops that they cannot and will not agree to take on any additional parishes as their even older colleagues retire or die.

The second analysis lays the responsibility very largely on this generation of older priests. According to one bishop (who is having some success in fostering vocations in his own diocese), they – and with them some of the older bishops – have given way to a spirit of defeatism and created in France the phenomenon of the 'invisibility of the clergy', of which a telling symbol has been their refusal to wear any form of distinctive clerical dress or even a cross in their lapel. If these priests have no belief, pride or confidence in their own calling and prefer to work in 'the real world' outside all the structures of the Church, how – it is asked – can they be in a position to encourage vocations to the priesthood among the young?

It is impossible to reconcile these two analyses.[2] One bishop – now retired – has, however, put his finger on a point that is absolutely crucial. His former diocese was largely rural and very de-christianized (indeed, when asked by Archbishop Michael Ramsey if he had many non-Catholic Christians in his diocese, he replied, without a moment's hesitation, 'No, but lots of non-Christian Catholics!'). According to him, there is no lack of a spirit of generosity and self-sacrifice among the rising generation of committed Christian young men, many of whom are being drawn to some of the strictest of the religious orders. Celibacy is a problem (and this particular bishop is not alone in being ready to envisage the ordination of married men), but even more of a problem is the loneliness that so many of the rural clergy – at some distance from their nearest colleague and with few practising Catholics in their parishes – have to endure. *The Communauté St-Martin* – amongst others – aims to deal precisely with this problem.

The Distinctive Diaconate

In 1969 the first ordinations to the permanent (or distinctive) diaconate took place, after the Second Vatican Council had made this once again a possibility. By the end of 1993, 902 permanent deacons had been ordained. 90% of these men are married, and they are either in some form of full-time employment or retired. None are ordained under the age of 35, and it is understood that in the first place their diaconal service has to be lived out in the context of their working and family lives. Nevertheless, all of them are ordained for a diocese and have a role to play in the mission of the Church in their diocese. The diminution of the number of priests and the fact that an increasing number of permanent deacons have now themselves retired from their paid employment are both contributing to the fact that they are taking on a much more visible and active role in the parishes, of which they often have the pastoral charge.

Sunday Worship without a Priest

The shortage of priests has led to a new phenomenon in French churches, the ADAP (*assemblée dominicale en l'absence de prêtre*) – Sunday worship in the absence of a priest. This does not usually take place more than once a month, but in some rare instances can occur on four Sundays out of five. The service in question is a Liturgy of the Word followed by distribution of Holy Communion from the Reserved Sacrament, presided over by a deacon, a religious (sister) or an authorized lay person, aided by a

---

2   Nevertheless, a recent publication from the Bishops' Bureau of Doctrinal Studies, *Les ministres ordonnés dans une Eglise-communion* – Ordained Ministers in a Church which is Communion (Paris, 1993), does provide a searching, serene and objective theological reflection on the whole issue.

A laywoman – permanente en pastorale (authorized full-time lay assistant) – presides over an ADAP

team who help to prepare and 'animate' the service. The provision of an ADAP has certain clear advantages, allowing congregations to meet every week (with or without a priest), allowing for them to receive the Blessed Sacrament and developing the pastoral and liturgical responsibility of the laity. The bishops are, however, aware of the risks and ambiguities of the exercise.[3] Confusion exists both about the Eucharist (revealingly disclosed in the not uncommon but highly inaccurate phrase *messe sans prêtre*) and also about the pastoral role of the priest (obscured when the visiting priest is rushing from one mass to another or has no real pastoral relationship with the congregation in question).

The Religious Communities

It is difficult for English people whose memories of France (either in real life or as portrayed on the screen) go back some way to envisage a France without monasteries and convents; without sisters in the streets, the *Métro* and the buses, in schools and in churches; without such great monastic centres as Solesmes. Some acquaintance with the complex historical background will, however, remind us that the religious life was completely suppressed during the Revolution, that it was with great difficulty restored in the nineteenth century, and that in order to survive at all many of the orders had to take the road of exile during the struggles surrounding the Separation of Church and

---

[3]   Cf. *Les ministres ordonnés dans une Eglise-communion (op. cit.)*.

State. So it was, for example, that the monks of Solesmes came to Quarr on the Isle of Wight and that the young Jesuit, Pierre Teilhard de Chardin, had to spend so many of his years of study in Jersey and in Hastings. It took time for the religious life in all its forms to be accepted again in France and in many cases – as at Bec – the return of the monks to some of the historic abbeys only took place after the Second World War.

The Men's Orders

In the ten years from 1980 to January 1991 the number of French male religious dropped from 18,128 to 15,155. The category most affected by this drop has been that of the active orders and clerical congregations; the orders least affected have been those of monks (Benedictines, Cistercians, etc), of whom there were 1,610 in 1980 and 1,603 in 1991. Perhaps the most gravely affected of all have been the missionary congregations, which were formerly very numerous – in Africa and in Asia in particular. Some of the most flourishing, on the other hand, have been a number of the more conservative Benedictine monasteries.

Among the signs of vitality and hope have been not only recent indications of more vocations to the religious life and real reform and renewal of the rules and spirit of the different historic orders, but also the creation of new orders or new forms of religious life. The *Communauté St-Jean* is one of the best known of the new orders. It was founded by Marie-Dominique Philippe, a professor at the University of Fribourg, and a group of his students in 1975; it now has three hundred brothers in thirty-two houses in thirteen countries, as well as about fifty contemplative sisters in five convents and nearly one hundred 'apostolic sisters' in eight different houses. Another experiment has been a kind of urban monasticism (in Paris, Lyon and Aix-en-Provence, for example) which has tried to ally the contemplative and monastic vocation with a presence in the heart of the great cities and a liturgical apostolate in churches like St-Gervais in Paris, St-Nizier in Lyon and St-Jean-de-Malte in Aix. This has often gone hand in hand with the rediscovery of what could be called 'episcopal monasticism', communities of monks (and often, as in the case of the Paris-based *Communautés de Jérusalem*, nuns as well) which put themselves under the direct authority of the diocesan bishop. More and more lay people are being attracted to worship in these and other great monastic churches, drawn – as many Anglicans in England are drawn to the cathedrals of their land – by the quality of the liturgy, the music and the preaching and by the atmosphere of prayer.

The Womens' Orders

The same crisis is apparent here as among the secular clergy and the active religious orders for men. By 1990 only 8% of religious sisters were under 50 years of age, although at the most recent count the total number of sisters in active communities – *religieuses de vie apostolique* – was 56,695. Great changes have taken place among the communities – *congrégations* – and not only in such questions as the modification or

The offertory procession at a national gathering of religious sisters

abandonment of the habit and the reform and renewal of their rules and constitutions. Women are now usually older when they come to try their vocation, and already have some experience of a job or profession in the secular world. Sisters, too, are increasingly exercising roles of considerable responsibility, not only within their communities or within the traditional spheres of education and care of the sick but also in the wider life of the Church; some are in charge of parishes because of the even greater shortage of priests.

The most recent figures indicate that there are in addition 6,372 nuns – *moniales* – in contemplative communities, and that the crisis of vocations is far less acute here than it is for the *religieuses de vie apostolique*. The *moniales* belong not only to the classic and historic orders, such as the Benedictines and Carmelites, but also to some new orders such as that of the *Soeurs de Bethléem* (which also has a male branch), known not only for the quality of its art work but for its presence at a number of historic sites, much visited by tourists, such as the Abbey of Le Thoronet in the Var.

English visitors should be aware of a potentially confusing difference of vocabulary in France. In French the word *monastère* (monastery) can be used to describe a house of nuns as well as a house of monks and the word *couvent* (convent) is used not only to describe a house of sisters but also a house of Dominican friars – as in the Couvent St-Jacques in Paris.

The 'New Communities' and the Charismatic Renewal

The term *Le Renouveau* (the Renewal) is widely used in the French Church today, but without any precise definition or any precise frontiers. It is used to describe a phenomenon which has its origins in the Charismatic Renewal and which began to make itself felt in France in the early 1970s, covering both *groupes de prière* (prayer groups) and the new-style communities which in many cases grew out of them. More generally, however, the phrase 'the Renewal' and the phrase the 'new communities' are used to include some communities which have a slightly earlier history and which have only indirect links with the Charismatic Renewal. One such community, for example, is *L'Arche*, founded in France in 1964 by the French Canadian layman Jean Vanier. It works among the mentally handicapped and has branches all over the world, including a number of houses in the United Kingdom.[4] Jean Vanier's spiritual guide was Fr Thomas Philippe, whose own brother, Marie-Dominique Philippe, like him a priest and a Dominican, founded the *Communauté St-Jean*. Another example is that of the Abbé Pierre, the outspoken champion of the homeless and the outcast, and his Companions of Emmaus.

It is surely no coincidence that it was shortly after the radical challenge of the *événements* of May 1968 that the Charismatic Renewal began to manifest itself within the Catholic Church in France, partly in reaction against the spirit of May 1968 but also in reaction to what was felt to be largely responsible for that revolt – aridity and lack of spirituality and warmth within the Church. Other inspirations have been the Ecumenical Movement (for some of the new communities are interconfessional and elements in the spirituality and liturgy of the Eastern churches – such as icons and Eastern-style singing – are often prominent features in their worship), and the influence of the so-called 'base communities' of Latin America, with their concern for the poor, the marginalized and the handicapped. The variety of influences and the fact that the new communities are all very different from one another make the phenomenon (it is doubtful if one should talk of a 'movement'; the phrase *un courant spirituel* – a spiritual trend – is often used instead) difficult to label for those who want to register it on a traditionalist-progressive scale. Those outside the Renewal see its rediscovery of certain traditional devotions, such as Adoration of the Blessed Sacrament, and the high degree of personal authority given to many of its leaders as putting it on the 'right'; others see its bias to the poor, the prominent role it gives to the laity and its adoption of Pentecostalist practices, such as speaking in tongues, as putting it on the 'left'.

The Renewal began with the *groupes de prière,* and these still involve more people (more than 1,750 groups altogether in France) than the communities. The groups are often quite small and informal, but certain summer gatherings, notably the one held at Paray-le-Monial, bring together thousands of people, young people in particular.

The 'New Communities' have grown out of the prayer groups and are basically of two main types, *communautés d'alliance* (covenant communities) and *communautés de vie*

---

4   Cf. Kathryn Spink, *Jean Vanier and l'Arche* (London, 1990).

(life communities). The former (including some of the best known such as *l'Emmanuel* and *le Chemin Neuf*) do have some of their members living a common life in the same house, but on the whole they have their own homes and live out their apostolate in their daily life and work, meeting regularly for prayer and mutual support. Different degrees of commitment are possible and among the members are married couples, priests and lay people and some pledged to celibacy. The *communautés de vie* are more monastic in style, with vows similar to the traditional religious vows, involving life-long commitment and with a vocation to contemplative prayer. They do often, however, contain married couples and their children as well as men and women who have taken a vow of celibacy. An Anglican is struck by the historic parallel of Nicholas Ferrar and the seventeenth-century community of Little Gidding, but this particular precedent seems to be unknown to the French communities.

It is very often the case that the leader of a community or the head of one of its houses, known as the *Berger* or Shepherd, is a member of the laity, although there may be one or more priests among the members. There were perhaps many reasons why the majority of French Catholics – and notably the bishops – looked with some wariness at this whole phenomenon at the outset; they were not happy about its alleged emotionalism and its pentecostal style. One bishop has confessed, however, that although it was something of a shock for him to discover that he had to discuss the ministry of a priest who was a member of a community in his diocese with a lay *Berger*, he now sees this as both normal and healthy. A number of bishops (Mgr Gaidon, Bishop of Cahors, and Mgr de Monléon, Bishop of Pamiers, among them) have themselves been influenced – as of course was Cardinal Suenens, the former Belgian Primate – by the Renewal, and there are now both a *Groupe épiscopal pour le Renouveau charismatique*, chaired by the Archbishop of Albi, and diocesan delegates in most dioceses responsible for liaison between the communities and the bishops. The fact that these communities profess a real and deep loyalty to the Church and are encouraging so many vocations to the priesthood has done much to transform the attitude of the episcopate, even though many French Catholics and many of the older clergy in particular are still extremely reticent about them.[5]

The Laity

The Church in France has for long been served by distinguished lay men and women of high intellectual and spiritual quality and with real commitment to the Church's mission in the world. For a long time they were drawn to be 'militants' in specifically Catholic movements in the political, social and trades union world [6] or in specifically Catholic branches of organizations such as the Scouts and Guides. Another way in which the specifically lay apostolate has been lived out has been in the movements of Catholic

---

[5]   I am indebted to 'The New Communities in France', a 1992 sabbatical project by Charles and Felicity Handley, for some of the information in this section.

[6]   See p.25 above.

Trinity and Emmanuel: A parish in the heart of Paris confided to a Community of the Renewal

The Church of the Holy Trinity in the ninth arrondissement, close to the Gare St-Lazare and the Opéra, is one of the most spacious, monumental and sumptuous of the churches of central Paris built during the reign of Napoleon III – 'une église élégante et commode' was how one contemporary described it. The parish still has many residents, but it is above all a business and commercial area and includes part of Pigalle – the Soho of Paris. The church contains one of the finest Cavaillé-Coll organs, and from 1931 until his death in 1992 its *titulaire* was none other than Olivier Messiaen.

In 1986 La Trinité became the first of two parishes to be confided by Cardinal Lustiger to the *Communauté de l'Emmanuel*; Père Francis Kohn, a priest of the Community, became its Curé. The life of the parish today is one of great vitality; the average attendance on a Sunday (counting all the masses both in the Parish Church and in the Chapel of St Rita) is about 2,500; the average attendance on weekdays about 300. A visitor looking in on a Sunday in January might find a full crypt at 10.30 for a family Mass, particularly adapted to the needs of families with young children. It is difficult to find a spare seat in the packed nave upstairs at 11.30 for the High Mass, attended by a varied congregation with a large proportion of young people, celebrated in a style which combines traditional liturgical dignity (a full team of servers with cross, lights and incense), fine organ music and simple chants which enable everyone to participate.

As a Community of the Charismatic Renewal, the team at La Trinité has tried to strike a balance, neither imposing its own particular style on the congregation as a whole nor trying to hide the specific gifts and charisms which constitute the dynamic of its own life, but providing opportunities for those who wish to do so to share in them.

L'Emmanuel is fully aware of the particular needs of the area it serves in the parish and tries to meet them positively and imaginatively. Among its initiatives are its restaurant in Pigalle, *Le Bistrot du Curé*, which allows it to make contact with many who would never darken the doors of a church; the daily provision on weekdays in the crypt with the help of 120 volunteers of a free, hot meal for over 300 disadvantaged or homeless people; and the opening in January 1994 of a new parish centre – DCT (*'Du Côté de la Trinité'*) with cafeteria, bookshop and meeting rooms.

The logo of the Emmanuel Community

Action, particularly in the specialized groups aimed at a well-defined section of the community. The work of a remarkable Belgian priest, the Abbé Joseph Cardijn (created a cardinal in 1965), in launching the JOC (*Jeunesse ouvrière chrétienne* – Young Christian Workers) in 1925 soon caught on in France, where it was introduced in 1927 by the Abbé Guérin, a curate in the working-class suburb of Clichy. Today it may not have all the momentum it once had, but in 1990 it could still rally a crowd of 100,000 at La Courneuve. Parallel to the JOC (and the *jocistes*) are other branches of Catholic Action such as the JIC (*Jeunesse indépendante chrétienne*), aimed at the bourgeoisie, the JEC (*Jeunesse étudiante chrétienne*), aimed at students, and the MRJC (*Mouvement rural de jeunesse chrétienne*), aimed at the rural community, and other branches too for those no longer young, such as ACI (*Action catholique des Milieux indépendants*) and ACO (*Action catholique ouvrière*). The point of this specialization is neither snobbery nor allegiance to the theory of the class war; rather, that it is the vocation of Christians in a particular *milieu* to penetrate and evangelize that *milieu*.

Today, however, there is a widespread feeling that Catholic Action reached its peak some time ago and that the lay vocation is finding new directions to follow. The shortage of priests has had two results, one clearly and unambiguously positive, the other more problematical. For too long in the parishes the clergy did – or at least ran – everything themselves; now, increasingly, far more in the spheres of liturgy, finance, catechesis and education is being taken over by the laity, together with a bigger share in pastoral and missionary responsibility. This de-clericalization of the Church's structures is wholly positive, as is the remarkable increase in the number of the laity studying theology. What is problematical is the fact that with a specific episcopal mandate or *envoi en mission* some lay people are having to assume a large part of the pastoral ministry of the clergy, including the pastoral care of parishes (although in theory a priest with the title of *modérateur* supervises those parishes confided to a lay *animateur* or *animatrice*). In some dioceses it is estimated that there is one such *permanent laïque* or *animateur pastoral* (often in fact a woman – *une permanente* or *une animatrice*) for every three priests. The problem is, of course, the grave risk of distortion in the understanding of the specific roles of priests (in danger of being defined exclusively in terms of those sacraments which they alone can celebrate), deacons and lay people and in the theological understanding of pastoral ministry. The problem is, at the deepest level, a problem of ecclesiology.[7] To point this out is not in any way to begrudge the laity their newly found role of shared responsibility within and for the Church; rather, it is to issue a warning that there is now the real risk of a dangerous slide from co-responsibility to confusion.

New Christians

Of all the signs of hope for the future of the Catholic Church in France none can be more significant than the striking increase in the number of adult baptisms and the rapid

---

7   See the penetrating analysis by Fr Bernard Sesboüé, 'Les animateurs pastoraux laïcs; une prospective théologique', in *Etudes*, September 1992.

growth and development of the catechumenate under the direction of the *Service National du Catéchuménat* and the *Service du Catéchuménat* in each diocese.

The average length of the catechumenate is two years. At present there are over 10,000 lay Christians who act as *'accompagnateurs'* – sponsoring, befriending and 'accompanying' the new converts on their journey of faith. This journey is marked by three distinct moments: firstly, enrolment as a catechumen; secondly, the call or election to baptism – *l'appel définitif* – usually on the first Sunday in Lent; thirdly, the celebration of the Sacraments of Initiation, normally at the Easter Vigil.

In 1976 there were 890 catechumens, in 1980 4,006, in 1991 5,643 and in 1993 8,430. It is reckoned that in 1995 there are about 9,000 and that the number is increasing at the rate of about 25% *per annum*. About three quarters of the candidates are between 20 and 40 years old, two-thirds of them are women and three-quarters claim to have had no previous religious affiliation of any kind but to be discovering faith in God and in Christ for the first time.

Postscript: *L'Affaire Gaillot*

In January 1995 Mgr Jacques Gaillot, Bishop of Evreux, was summoned to the Vatican by Cardinal Gantin, Prefect of the Congregation for Bishops. The outcome of the interview was that he was dismissed or removed from his see, technically by being translated from his real diocese of Evreux in Normandy to a titular see in North Africa. It was a disciplinary sanction, but he remains a member of the college of bishops. Although the abruptness of the decision was a shock and a surprise even to Mgr Gaillot's colleagues in the French episcopate, it was not totally unexpected, since both the present President of the Episcopal Conference (Mgr Duval) and his predecessor (the late Cardinal Decourtray) had taken issue with him publicly in recent years and exhorted him to behave in a more 'collegial' fashion. Many observers who cannot be accused of theological conservatism have remarked that he seemed bent on provoking the kind of confrontation that could only have one outcome.

Nevertheless, the news of Mgr Gaillot's deprivation caused shock waves that were felt throughout France and far beyond, provoking protests and demonstrations and drawing a crowd of 20-30,000 for his last mass as bishop in Evreux. Many even of those who had criticized him quite vigorously were seriously disturbed at the way he was treated and sent messages of sympathy. A number of his fellow bishops took part in his farewell mass, others questioned sharply the procedures by which he was judged, and the episcopate as a whole has made itself responsible for finding him a continuing ministry in the French Church.

The *affaire Gaillot* has brought to the surface a number of paradoxes. One of the major charges against him was his failure to act collegially, but a failure in collegiality is also one of the accusations levelled at the way in which he was treated at Rome. Again – as one French bishop has remarked – if it can be said that Mgr Gaillot was often singularly '*maladroit*' in his attitudes and in his behaviour, it has to be said that the Vatican's handling of the affair has also been maladroit. Finally, however, Mgr Gaillot, unlike Mgr Lefebvre, has no intention of allowing a schism to gather round his name; the Church, he assured his supporters, remains his family and he remains clearly within its communion.

The cross of Canterbury set into the wall of the Abbey Church at Bec at the time of its consecration, 1 November 1969.

IV 'THE FRENCH CONNECTION': ECUMENICAL DIALOGUE BETWEEN ANGLICANS AND FRENCH CATHOLICS

A plaque in the Benedictine Abbey of Notre-Dame du Bec-Hellouin in Normandy, put up in 1966 to commemorate the Battle of Hastings, touchingly and delicately evokes the memory of all the Normans of France and England who over many centuries died in battle *face à face ou côte à côte*, face to face or side by side. More widely and more generally, one can speak of the peoples of France and England as sharing a common history and as involved in a common destiny *face à face ou côte à côte*. This is true not least of relations between the churches in France and in England, marked at times by hostility and confrontation but more often, and especially more recently, by mutual sympathy, support and emulation.

During the Middle Ages there were particularly close and intimate links between the Church in England and the Church in France, especially during the eleventh and twelfth centuries. The traffic was not entirely one way; John of Salisbury, for example, who had been Secretary to St Thomas à Becket and attended him to Canterbury Cathedral on the day of his martyrdom in 1170, was Bishop of Chartres from 1176 until his death in 1180. These close links were almost completely breached when, to quote a former Chancellor of Chichester Cathedral, Canon Cheslyn Jones, Henry VIII 'took the Church of England out of Europe'.

Anglicans in France

Anglican worship has, however, been celebrated in France from the sixteenth century onwards, initially only in the private chapel of the English Ambassador, conducted by his chaplain. One of the first of these was Richard Hakluyt (d. 1616), who served in Paris from 1583 to 1588 and eventually became Archdeacon of Westminster. He was apparently so angered by taunts that the English had achieved little in the way of trade and discovery that he published in 1589 his *Principal Navigations, Voyages and Discoveries of the English Nation* to vindicate the honour of his fellow-countrymen.

Paris and St-Germain-en-Laye (to the west of Paris) became notable centres of Anglican worship after the outbreak of the Civil War in England led to the overthrow of the Church of England, its episcopate and its liturgy, and eventually to the execution of Charles I in 1649. Many exiles gathered around the court of Queen Henrietta Maria – herself, of course, both Roman Catholic and French – and for a time during the Commonwealth both Charles II and his brother, the future James II, also lived in Paris or St-Germain-en-Laye. In 1644 the deprived Master of Peterhouse, Cambridge, and Dean of Peterborough, John Cosin (to become Bishop of Durham in 1660 and to take a leading part in the revision of the Book of Common Prayer in 1661-2) came to France to be Chaplain to the Anglican members of the Queen's household. He had a difficult and delicate task, especially after the death of Charles I when the Queen intensified her efforts to convert her children and her household to the Roman allegiance. Among his other tasks Dr Cosin had to help 'certain ladys of great qualitie who were then to be discharged from our Queen Mother's service unless they would go over to the Roman masse'. Many other eminent divines, including John Bramhall (the future Archbishop of Armagh) and George Morley (the future Bishop of Winchester), seem to have ministered in Paris during this period, and Thomas Sydserff, Bishop of Galloway, conducted ordinations. A description of an ordination by the Bishop of Galloway was given by the diarist John Evelyn. It took place in the private chapel of the 'English Resident' (the representative of the exiled King Charles II during the Commonwealth), Sir Richard Browne, John Evelyn's father-in-law. The Resident's Chapel was the centre in Paris for Anglican worship during this difficult time; after the Restoration Anglican worship was once more celebrated in the Chapel of the Ambassador.

It was in July 1682 that William Wake, a young priest ordained only that March, arrived in Paris to take up his appointment as Chaplain to the Ambassador of Charles II. He must be considered as the most distinguished chaplain in the whole history of the Anglican presence in France: at any rate he is the only one to have ended up as Archbishop of Canterbury. He only remained in France until September 1685, but his short stay was both active and fruitful. Over and above his pastoral activity he made many friends among French Catholics and Protestants and attended both Catholic and Protestant services in a critical but appreciative spirit. He even dared to enter into controversy with the great Bossuet, 'The Eagle of Meaux', and was hailed enthusiastically in England as a 'young David... raised up... to slay the French Goliath'.

After the 1688 Revolution the exiled James II established his court at St-Germain-en-Laye; services for his Anglican supporters were known to have been conducted by – among others – the deprived Dean of Durham, Denis Granville. This policy was continued by King James II's son, 'the Old Pretender', both at St-Germain and at Bar-le-Duc in Lorraine; his Anglican Chaplain was the Irishman Charles Leslie. George Hickes, the deprived Dean of Worcester, was received by King James at St-Germain and nominated by him as Bishop of Thetford in order to continue the succession of the Nonjuring Bishops in England. King James informed Hickes that he had consulted the Pope, the Archbishop of Paris and the Bishop of Meaux (Bossuet), who had all encouraged him to nominate bishops. At the same time he nominated Thomas Wagstaffe as Bishop of Ipswich; the two were secretly consecrated by the deprived Bishops of Ely, Norwich and Peterborough at Enfield.

Early Ecumenical Dialogue

The story of Anglo-French ecumenical initiatives really begins in the nineteenth century, but there is nonetheless a pre-history which deserves some attention. It begins in the seventeenth century with Richard Montague, Bishop of Chichester, an advanced

William Wake, Archbishop of Canterbury from 1716 to 1737 (portrait at Lambeth Palace by I. Whood, 1736)

Laudian. He suggested to Gregorio Panzani, the papal envoy to the Court of Charles I, that it would be a good idea to organize bilateral theological conversations in France, since he was convinced that one would find there a more irenic climate for theological dialogue than would be possible in England. And at the very end of that seventeenth century two solid and massively learned works of George Bull, Bishop of St Davids, in defence of the Nicene faith elicited the approval of Bishop Bossuet and an official letter of thanks from the synod of the French clergy assembled at St Germain.

The eighteenth century for its part was to offer the astonishing spectacle of a correspondence between William Wake, who became Archbishop of Canterbury in 1716, and two Gallican theologians of the Sorbonne (the theological faculty of the University of Paris), Doctors Du Pin and Girardin, which explored the possibilities of reunion.[1] Wake had been prepared for this correspondence by his period in Paris and contacts he had made at that time. William Beauvoir, Chaplain to the British Ambassador, was very closely involved. Knowing that talk of a union was in the air, Parisians became curious and started attending Anglican services in some number. So Beauvoir could write to the Archbishop:

> Last Sunday we had a large congregation, and among them a curé in his usual habit, who behaved himself with decency and even edified our people. He is charmed with the way of worship in our Church, and wishes it to be introduced in all Christian churches. I knew him two years ago our bitter enemy, but is become our friend because he is better informed. I have dispersed a great many Common Prayer Books gratis among the clergy and others.

The authorities seem to have taken alarm at this turn of events: 'They threaten', wrote Beauvoir to the Archbishop, 'to suffer no French to resort to our congregations, and to place Guards within twenty paces of our Hotel [i.e. the Ambassador's residence], to take up those that come to it upon Sundays'.

In the light of all the ambiguities of that first dialogue – its political context which should never be forgotten, Wake's isolation (nobody else in the Church of England, none of his fellow bishops even, knew what he was doing), the mixed motives on both sides – we need to ask whether the goal was really reunion or whether it was on one side the idea of detaching the *Ecclesia Gallicana* from Rome and making it an independent national church like the Church of England, and on the other side the desire simply to bring the Church of England back into submission to Rome. In spite of all those ambiguities, Dr Henry McAdoo, Co-Chairman of ARCIC I, was able to see it as in some ways the pioneering and positive beginning of Anglican - Roman Catholic dialogue, because the major themes were explored in an irenic way for the first time in the course of this correspondence.

---

[1] The whole of this correspondence has been published by a French priest historian, Jacques Grès-Gayer, in *Paris-Cantorbéry (1717-1720), Le Dossier d'un Premier Oecuménisme* (Paris, 1989).

The Nineteenth Century

If the overwhelming majority of eighteenth-century Anglicans remained profoundly anti-Roman, we can, however, note a slight change of attitude with the arrival in England among the *émigrés* of clerical refugees from the fury of the French Revolution. Two bishops of the Church of England, the Bishops of London and Durham, sat on a Committee of Welcome to look after these refugee bishops and priests. In addition, Charles Lloyd, a future Bishop of Oxford, acknowledged that his interest in the Breviary was due entirely to his friendship with a group of French *émigré* priests who said their office together in a London chapel. He was later, during his time as Regius Professor of Divinity at Oxford, to deliver a course of lectures on the Book of Common Prayer which reflected that interest and which was to have influence on such prominent Tractarians as Pusey, Newman, Hurrell Froude and Robert Wilberforce. Moreover, a young layman, Ambrose Phillipps de Lisle, who became a Roman Catholic in 1825, attributed his conversion to Rome very largely to the influence of a French priest who taught him French at school, though he was careful to emphasize that the priest abstained from all proselytizing and did not work at all for his conversion. Phillipps de Lisle became an enthusiastic supporter – in a way that was sometimes perceived as embarrassing rather than helpful – of the Oxford Movement, and it was through his influence that in 1841 an anonymous letter from 'a member of the University of Oxford' (probably Newman's friend Dalgairns) was published in the French Catholic journal *L'Univers*. This letter had a considerable effect. A number of French clerics began to visit Oxford and to enthuse over Evensong in Magdalen College Chapel, and several theologians, among them the great Dominican, Lacordaire, were, at the instigation of Phillipps de Lisle, received by Newman. In the end Newman had to beg Phillipps de Lisle not to bring any more French priests to Oxford to see him because their presence was being misinterpreted.

Later, in the 1860s, after Newman had left the Church of England and the leadership of the Tractarians had passed to Dr Pusey, we find evidence of very strong links between Dr Pusey and several French-speaking Catholics. Pusey was not only translating and adapting French works of theology and spirituality, but was also visiting convents in France and Belgium in order to deepen his practical knowledge of the religious life – for the benefit of the new religious communities for women in the Church of England of which he was the founder or spiritual director. In the course of these visits he became friendly with Darboy, Archbishop of Paris, and Dupanloup, Bishop of Orléans, both leaders of what was called the 'Inopportunist' party, which was to oppose the definition of Papal Infallibility at Vatican I, and he also became acquainted with a Belgian Jesuit, Victor de Buck.[2] Pusey was working on his first *Eirenicon* and in it he explicitly referred to the dialogue between Wake and the Gallicans and evoked its positive spirit. Darboy also received the Bishop of Brechin, A.P. Forbes, the leading Scottish Tractarian. This led Fr de Buck to launch the ingenious but dangerously unrealistic idea that Forbes should go to the Council as an observer with Pusey as his *peritus*. Pusey

---

[2]   At some points in this chapter it is essential to refer to the Belgian contribution, in view of the close partnership between French and Belgian Catholics in the events here described.

however had no illusions. 'What can we expect', he wrote, 'when they invited the great Greek Church simply to submit? I expect nothing under the present Pope [he was referring to Pius IX]; under a future Pope there may be great changes'.

In 1884 a fateful meeting took place on the island of Madeira (which 40 years earlier had already seen a meeting between John Mason Neale and Montalembert which had begun fruitfully but had led nowhere). In that year an eminent English and Anglican aristocrat, Charles Lindley Wood (1839-1934), soon to become the second Viscount Halifax, and a French Lazarist priest of the humblest social origins, Fernand Portal (1855-1926), met. They were both in Madeira for reasons of health; Portal because of his own health, Halifax because of that of one of his sons. They were soon to become the staunchest and closest of friends for the rest of their lives. The celebrated *Campagne Anglo-Romaine* was conceived and planned in the course of their frequent long walks together in Madeira that winter, and the two friends were able when they got home to enlist some of the best minds and finest spirits of the Churches of France and England to take part in this campaign and to write for their monthly bulletin, *La Revue Anglo-Romaine*, consecrated entirely to the cause of Anglican-Roman Catholic reconciliation. They were led, mistakenly as we now see, to the idea that it would be good to begin the dialogue with what they thought was a neutral, factual and therefore relatively 'safe' subject, the question of Anglican Orders; this was taken up by Rome and provoked heavy opposition from the formidable trio of Cardinal Vaughan of Westminster, Dom Aidan Gasquet of Downside and Mgr Raphael Merry del Val in Rome, who succeeded in obtaining from Leo XIII in 1896 the Bull *Apostolicae Curae*, condemning Anglican Orders. The condemnation was of course a tragic and severe blow to Anglican - Roman Catholic reconciliation, and it killed both the Campaign and the Review. The two friends, however, refused to give up. 'Un jour', wrote Halifax to Portal, 'on verra que nous avions raison' – 'One day they will see that we were right'.

Malines and After

Portal and Halifax did not give up, they simply lay low – Portal of necessity, since he had earned the relentless hatred of Merry del Val and was to suffer for it. They waited from 1896 until 1921. In that year they travelled together to Belgium to visit the prestigious Archbishop of Malines and Primate of Belgium, Cardinal Mercier, who had shocked and scandalized Rome by going to a meeting of the Convention of the Episcopal Church of the United States when he was in America – earning him a letter of rebuke from Pope Benedict XV imforming him that it was 'regrettable' that he had agreed to meet 'the Episcopalian pseudo-bishops' and 'inadmissible' that he had called them 'brothers in the Christian faith'. Mercier had been sent a copy of the 1920 Lambeth Conference's *Appeal to all Christian People* by Archbishop Davidson. From this visit to Malines were born the Malines Conversations, regarded with a mixture of goodwill, nervousness and misgiving by both Pope and Archbishop of Canterbury at different stages of the Conversations, and with hostility by many Anglicans and by many Roman Catholics, especially English Roman Catholics. The participants were on the one side all either French or Belgian, though there was an abortive attempt to enlist an English

Cardinal Mercier
1851—1926

Lord Halifax
7 June 1839—19 January 1934

L'Abbé Portal
1855—1926

A card produced by the Church Union for the celebrations in 1984 of the 50th anniversary of the death of Lord Halifax

member, and on the other side all the Anglicans were high churchmen, though Bishop Charles Gore was far too liberal and anti-Roman for Halifax's taste. The dialogue was notable for being a dialogue of friends, people who came to know each other, trust each other, sympathize with each other and listen to each other. It was not a disputation, a negotiation or a bargaining, and though it was doomed to failure after Mercier's death, it remains a positive and significant milestone in the history of Anglican - Roman Catholic relations.

The dialogue also led to a very particular vision, encapsulated in the title of a memoir prepared for Cardinal Mercier by the Belgian Benedictine, Dom Lambert Beauduin (1873-1960): *L'Eglise Anglicane unie non absorbée* – the Church of England united not absorbed. This daring essay was to earn Dom Lambert a sentence of banishment (to France, which is not quite Siberia!) from the monastery of the Community of the Monks of Unity, which he had founded, which was only revoked in 1951. Its title, however, was appropriated half a century later by Paul VI in his address of welcome to Archbishop Donald Coggan in 1977: 'The pace of this movement has quickened marvellously in recent years, so that these words of hope, "The Anglican Church united not absorbed", are no longer a mere dream'. Dom Lambert Beauduin had founded the ecumenical review *Irénikon*, published by his monks and still flourishing – although threatened with suppression by the Roman authorities three times in its early years. It was with Dr Pusey in mind that M. Portal suggested the title to Dom Lambert.

The collapse of the Malines Conversations and the promulgation by Pius XI in 1928 of the Encyclical *Mortalium Animos*, which seemed to condemn unreservedly the Ecumenical Movement, ushered in another dark period. Two men kept alive the hope of better days to come – two French priests, to both of whom reference has already been made and both of whom, though their ecumenical vocations were very different,

The return from exile. Dom Lambert Beauduin at Chevetogne in 1954

acknowledged their debt to the Community of the Monks of Unity, founded by Dom Lambert Beauduin at Amay and now at Chevetogne in the Belgian Ardennes. These two priests actually met each other at Amay. One was Fr Yves Congar (1904-95), the Dominican theologian whose pioneer work *Chrétiens désunis*, published in 1937,[3] was the first serious study of the Ecumenical Movement by a Roman Catholic theologian. Dr Robert Runcie, Archbishop of Canterbury, visited him on his sick-bed during his visit to Paris in 1984 and conferred on him the Cross of St Augustine in recognition of his great services to Christian unity. Ten years later Pope John Paul II created him a Cardinal. The other priest was the founder (or perhaps, more strictly, the refounder) of the Week of Prayer for Christian Unity, a schoolmaster from Lyon, the Abbé Paul Couturier (1881-1953), who twice visited England before the Second World War and counted many Anglicans among his close friends. In their very different ways Congar and Couturier transmitted

something of the heritage of the Malines Conversations to succeeding generations – Congar through his studies, his intellectual researches and his influence on theologians and scholars and on the Second Vatican Council, Couturier through promoting the work of the Week of Prayer for Christian Unity and through his correspondence with Anglicans, particularly with enclosed religious communities, which encouraged a deep communion at the level of prayer for unity.

The Second Vatican Council

The Second Vatican Council (1962-65) inaugurated, of course, a new era. But although John XXIII's announcement of the Council to the assembled Cardinals in January 1959 was something of a bombshell, causing universal astonishment and provoking reactions either of elated hope or dismayed incredulity, it was not unprepared. It is not impossible that the Pope's decision was in part inspired by the man he had earlier referred to as 'my old Belgian friend', Dom Lambert Beauduin, and who had long been urging the vital necessity of another Council to complete and balance the unfinished and one-sided achievement of Vatican I.

Yves Congar in 1979 at the house of the Protestant deaconess community in Versailles

3   Translated into English as *Divided Christendom* (London, 1939).

Moreover, its ecumenical dimension had been discreetly prepared by a growing number of continental Roman Catholic theologians and ecumenists, so many of whom were French or Belgian.

In the preparatory period between the announcement and the inauguration of the Council the Anglican Communion took a lead in fostering this ecumenical dimension. In 1959 the Catholic University of Louvain welcomed the first of a succession of priest-students, appointed by the Archbishop of Canterbury on the recommendation of the Church of England Council on Foreign Relations, to study in its *schola maior* of theology. It was the first Roman Catholic faculty to make this gesture.[4] In 1960, the year when the Vatican Secretariat for Christian Unity was set up under the presidency of the newly-created German Jesuit Cardinal, Augustin Bea, the Archbishop of Canterbury, Dr Geoffrey Fisher, paid a call on Pope John. He was the first Archbishop of Canterbury to visit a Pope since the fourteenth century and the first ever leader of a non-Roman Catholic communion to do so. This led to the appointment of an Anglican representative in Rome to study the preparations for the Council and to act as a liaison with the Secretariat – another 'first'– and to yet another 'first' when the Anglican Communion took the lead in accepting an invitation to send observers to the Council.

This is not the place to recount the history of the Council, but in the context of Anglican - Roman Catholic rapprochement there are four points which need to be made.

First, there was the influence behind the scenes of a powerful group of French-speaking theologians and in particular of what the Italians came to call the *squadra belga* (the Belgian gang) of Cardinal Suenens, Mgr De Smedt (Bishop of Bruges) and the theologians of the University of Louvain, men like Philips, Thils, Moeller and Aubert. In 1942 the monks of Chevetogne and some theologians of Louvain had held the first of the Chevetogne *colloques oecuméniques*, which were to have – and continue to have – a wide and deep influence. Immediately after the war French theologians of the calibre of Congar, Daniélou and Dumont (of the Dominican ecumenical foundation *Istina*) began to take part, and non-Roman Catholic participants began to attend in 1947; the first Anglican to do so was the Revd Henry Brandreth of St George's, Paris. The volume which issued from the 1959 Colloquium, *Le Concile et les Conciles* (1960), was to have an enormous impact on the theology of Vatican II.

Secondly, there was the challenge to the draft *schemata* (in the drawing up of which conservative curialist influence had been dominant) delivered during the first session by a group of Belgian, French and German bishops – a challenge which was successful and therefore marked the crucial turning point of the Council. These bishops were not only better prepared than any other group but had a group of distinguished theologians (some of whom had been under a cloud in the previous pontificate) to act as their theological experts or *periti*. To this group must be added the name of Patriarch Maximos IV of Antioch, leader of the Eastern Rite Melkite Catholic Church in the Middle East. He was

---

[4]   The priest-students were: John Wilkinson, Martin Reardon, Roger Greenacre, David Keene, John Halliburton, Hugh Wybrew, David Miller and David Stonebanks.

a man who was greatly influenced by French theology and who always spoke in the Council in French, refusing to speak in Latin, the official language of the Council, because that was the language of the Western Church.

Thirdly, there was the key role played by the journalists at the Council, particularly by those from France and Belgium. The influence of the Curia was directed at revealing as little as possible about what was taking place either within the conciliar *aula* (St Peter's) or outside it. It was men like Henri Fesquet and Fr Antoine Wenger from Paris and Jan Grootaers from Brussels who made it their business to find out what was really going on and to publish it, so helping participants as well as non-participants to understand and making the Council much more of an open process than it would otherwise have been.

Fourthly, there was the considerable influence of France, its thinkers, artists, writers and philosophers, on the man who attended the first session of the Council as Cardinal Montini, Archbishop of Milan, and who in June 1963 was to succeed John XXIII as Pope Paul VI. One of his closest French friends was the layman Jean Guitton of the *Académie Française*, the first lay person to address a public session of the Council; they first met on 8 September 1950 and then met annually on the same date until Paul VI's death in 1978. Jean Guitton himself, while a student at the prestigious *Ecole Normale Supérieure*, had fallen under the spell of its chaplain, M. Portal, and had then become a close friend of Lord Halifax. Was it perhaps from Jean Guitton that Montini acquired an interest in Anglicanism, soon to be heightened when he received a visit from Dr Bell, Bishop of Chichester, and given notable expression when he entertained a group of five Anglicans in Milan for a ten day stay in the following year, 1956? Be that as it may, Paul VI has been described by Prof. Owen Chadwick as the first and indeed the only Pope who really understood the Church of England.[5] His commitment to ecumenism was no less heartfelt than John XXIII's, but embraced with deeper theological understanding.

ARCIC I

In 1966 the then Archbishop of Canterbury, Dr Michael Ramsey, paid an official visit to Pope Paul VI in Rome and signed with him a Common Declaration at St Paul's-without-the-Walls. It was on this occasion that Paul VI made one of the most significant of the symbolic gestures that marked his pontificate, when he slipped off his episcopal ring and gave it to Dr Ramsey. There was surely here a conscious reference to the gift by the dying Cardinal Mercier of his episcopal ring to Lord Halifax and another fruit of the Pope's friendship with Guitton. The Common Declaration committed the two Communions to formal dialogue. There was first of all a Joint Preparatory Commission, whose membership included two French theologians (one of whom, Louis Bouyer, was known personally by both the Pope, who suggested his name, and the Archbishop) and then the first Anglican - Roman Catholic International Commission, whose membership included three French Roman Catholics, George Tavard, Jean Tillard and Pierre Duprey

---

5   O. Chadwick, *Michael Ramsey: A Life* (Oxford, 1990), p.317.

(of whom the two latter still serve on the somewhat slimmer ARCIC II). More recently, a Belgian Catholic theologian from Leuven, Dr Adelbert Denaux, has been appointed to ARCIC II.

It is interesting to note that the texts of the ARCIC Agreed Statements all appeared in French translation very promptly after their publication in English, and that the French translation of the *Final Report* of ARCIC I was published in the same year as the official English text.[6] Even the Study Guide published by English ARC (the English Anglican - Roman Catholic Committee) came out two years later in French.[7] The invaluable French publication *La Documentation Catholique*, which publishes the complete text of important official and unofficial documents, has often given a large place to the publication of texts relating to Anglican - Roman Catholic dialogue. Other texts, together with related articles and commentaries, have been published in the French ecumenical review *Istina* and in the French-language Belgian ecumenical review *Irénikon*.

ARCIC I concluded its work in 1982 with the publication of its *Final Report*. At Pentecost of that year Pope John Paul II visited Canterbury and there signed with Dr Robert Runcie, Archbishop of Canterbury, a *Common Declaration* setting out the next steps to be taken in the dialogue, including a process of evaluation and reception of the Agreed Statements of ARCIC I. The *Final Report* was to be studied by each member church of the Anglican Communion in ways defined by its own synodical structures and by each Episcopal Conference of the Roman Catholic Church. In both cases a response was demanded to an identical question agreed beforehand by both sides – whether the Agreed Statements were 'consonant in substance' with (in one case) 'the faith of Anglicans' and (in the other case) with 'the faith of the Catholic Church'. The French analysis was both thorough and positive, and has been published in English as well as in French.[8] It is perhaps therefore not surprising that one of the most rigorous critiques of the official Roman Response to ARCIC I (published at the end of 1991 and generally perceived as very hard-line) has been that by the French Episcopal Commission for Christian Unity. In particular, it challenges the Roman Response for appearing totally to ignore the responses of bishops' conferences.[9]

Anglicans and Roman Catholics in France Today

French participation and interest in the work of ARCIC is far from exhausting French involvement in Anglican - Roman Catholic relations today. There are now 33 Church of England congregations in France, looked after by 23 priests, together with a number

---

[6]   *Jalons pour l'Unité* (Paris, 1982).

[7]   *Nouveaux Jalons pour l'Unité* (Paris, 1984).

[8]   English translation: *One in Christ*, xxi (1985), 329-48.

[9]   *Documents-Episcopat*, no. 5, March 1994. English translation in C. Hill and E. Yarnold (eds), *Anglicans and Roman Catholics: The Search for Unity* (London, 1994), pp.171-184.

of seasonal chaplaincies open for only part of the year (e.g. from Easter to September) and relying on the services of priests supplied from England or elsewhere. These chaplaincies – permanent and seasonal – form the Archdeaconry of France within the Church of England Diocese of Gibraltar in Europe. (In addition, there is a Pro-Cathedral in Paris belonging to the Convocation of American Episcopal Churches in Europe.)

The great 'population explosion' which brought British people to live in France (for pleasure as well as for business) had taken place after the Battle of Waterloo in 1815. Nine years afterwards the number of expatriate British residents in France was variously reckoned at between thirty and fifty thousand, with eight thousand of them in Paris alone. It is difficult to estimate the present size of the Anglican population in France.[10] The British consular service in Paris does have figures of the number of British nationals resident in France; these come from the French Ministry of the Interior and are calculated on the basis of those who have obtained a residence permit. The figures released for 1990 gave a total of 57,138 – a record increase (12.1%) on the 1989 total of 50,954. These 1990 statistics give a total of 24,298 British nationals for Paris and the Paris region – most of them in the western suburbs. The only other *département* with more than 2,000 was that of the Alpes-Maritimes on the French Riviera (3,500).

These figures would indicate that there must now be considerable numbers of at least nominal Anglicans living at an enormous distance from the nearest Anglican chaplain. Some of these might be expected to look more naturally to French Protestantism for pastoral and sacramental care, but there are numerous French dioceses which only contain one or two pastors and one or two congregations of the *Eglise Réformée de France* for the whole of their area. The diocese of Chartres, for example, which corresponds to the *département* of the Eure-et-Loir, has a congregation and a pastor of the *Eglise Réformée de France* in Chartres itself and a congregation in Dreux which has been for some time without a pastor of its own (with in one village a congregation and pastor of the *Eglise Evangélique Libre*). The diocese of Cahors, which corresponds to the *département* of the Lot, has no resident pastor of the Reformed Church within its territory at all – although one of the two pastors living in the neighbouring *département* of the Tarn-et-Garonne (Diocese of Montauban), where there are several Protestant communities, takes services in Cahors from time to time.

There are not a few examples of Anglicans who play a leading role in the life, worship and activity of French Catholic parishes and not a few couples in interchurch marriages (*foyers mixtes*) who also play such a role, sometimes also worshipping in the nearest Anglican chaplaincy on a more or less regular basis. It was this phenomenon of Anglicans living at a distance from the regular ministrations of their own Church which led French ARC (the French Anglican - Roman Catholic Committee), soon after its foundation in 1969, to ask the French bishops to accord to such Anglicans a measure of sacramental hospitality – principally, of course, eucharistic hospitality, but also the possibility of recourse to the sacraments of reconciliation (confession and absolution),

---

[10]   It is important to remember that not all British nationals are even nominal Anglicans and that not all Anglicans are citizens of the United Kingdom.

56

and of the anointing of the sick. Encouraged by the evidence for a substantial agreement on the doctrine of the Eucharist provided by the Windsor Agreement of 1971 (the first of the Agreed Statements of the *Final Report* of ARCIC I), the French bishops responded very positively to this request. It should be noted that this admission to Holy Communion is not automatic or global but related to particular pastoral situations: Anglicans on holiday in France who desire to take advantage of this hospitality, should, if possible, consult the parish priest or the celebrant of the mass beforehand.[11]

Until the Second Vatican Council Anglicans either had to build their own churches or worship in French Protestant churches, but today Anglican worship is conducted not only in churches of the *Eglise Réformée de France* (as in Fontainebleau) but in French Catholic churches or chapels (as in Caen and Strasbourg). The ecumenical involvement of the Anglican chaplaincies in France is considered important by the main French churches. This involvement goes back in some cases a long way, particularly in the case of St George's Paris; in 1907 M. Portal was present at the funeral requiem of its Chaplain, George Washington, who had no doubt played a modest role in the Campagne Anglo-Romaine. In 1969 the *Comité mixte Anglican - Catholique Romain de France* (French ARC) was founded. Although it does have some responsibility in the wider area of Anglican - Roman Catholic relations (encouraging exchanges between France and Great Britain and helping to make Anglicanism better understood in France), its primary mandate is to foster relations between the two communities in France. Its members are appointed on the one side by the French Episcopal Conference and on the other by the Bishop of Gibraltar in Europe and the bishop in charge of the Convocation of American Churches in Europe. The Anglicans in France are invited to send an observer to the annual Plenary Assembly of the French Episcopal Conference in Lourdes, and they have also taken up observer status in the *Conseil d'Eglises Chrétiennes en France* (Council of Christian Churches in France). Observer status was accorded, rather than full membership, only because neither the Bishop of Gibraltar nor his suffragan is resident in France.

Cross-Channel Contacts

Relationships between the Church of England and the Catholic Church in France are by no means limited to contacts within France. The last thirty years have also seen increasing cross-channel links. At the national level, visits have been exchanged between the Archbishops of Canterbury and the French episcopate. Archbishop Michael Ramsey began this process in 1967, when he visited the Abbey of Bec, Rouen and Paris. In Paris he not only worshipped with the Anglican community but gave a lecture to the *Institut Catholique* (and was awarded an honorary doctorate), was solemnly received at the Cathedral of Notre-Dame and met leaders of the Orthodox and Protestant churches. He paid two later visits to France, on one occasion to Sens and Lyon and on the other to Taizé. His example has been followed by his successors. Archbishop Donald Coggan

---

[11] Cf. *Twinnings and Exchanges. Guidelines proposed by the Anglican - Roman Catholic Committees of France and England* (London, 1990), pp.8-11.

visited Bec, Caen and Bayeux in 1977. Archbishop Robert Runcie visited Paris, Autun, Taizé, Lyon and Bec in 1984. He made a private visit to Bec in 1987 and visited Strasbourg in 1989. Archbishop George Carey visited Taizé in 1992 and Strasbourg in 1993, and made a retreat at Bec in 1994. These visits have been reciprocated. In 1970 Cardinal Marty and two other French bishops came to England and in September 1989 three French bishops, led by Cardinal Decourtray, Archbishop of Lyon, came on a pastoral visit to England, spending some time in Canterbury and some time in Birmingham in order to gain first hand experience of the Church of England at work and at prayer.

It is important to underline the fact that the agenda for these exchange visits was not dominated by purely theological questions, though discussion of the progress of Anglican - Roman Catholic dialogue was one important item on it. The main object was for two 'majority' churches in secularized modern Europe to share their pastoral and missionary concerns and to learn from each other's experience. Such sharing had been going on informally for some time – many Anglicans for example were anxious to learn from the experience of worker priests and the *Mission de France*. Pastoral and missionary concerns are not the only sphere for such mutual interest. In the realm of spirituality the ecumenical community of Taizé draws thousands of visitors from Great Britain every year (and young people in particular), while in the realm of theological studies there is a considerable degree of cross-fertilization. When the future Cardinal Jean Daniélou gave the formal address on behalf of the *Institut Catholique* at the ceremony in which Archbishop Ramsey was given a doctorate, he was building upon a mutual friendship and a mutual respect for each other's theological work which went back to the days of the first Patristic Conferences at Oxford.

The last thirty years have also seen an enormous increase in the number of French people spending time in Great Britain and in the number of British people spending time in France – an increase which the opening of the Channel Tunnel may further accelerate. One aspect of this has been the growth in church 'twinnings'. Some of these started on a purely secular basis between two cities, towns or villages and have since acquired a churchly dimension; others have been on a specifically churchly basis from the beginning. They vary in scale from links between dioceses to links between parishes. French ARC was aware from the beginning of its work both of the exciting possibilities of such twinnings and also of some of the dangers; in time it began to organize joint meetings with English ARC, and in 1990 the two Committees jointly produced a bilingual guide to such twinnings with useful advice about such things as joint worship and eucharistic sharing.[12] It is highly desirable that, wherever possible, both English Roman Catholic and French Reformed involvement should be encouraged from the outset.

There are now five diocesan links between Church of England and French Catholic dioceses. The link between Chichester and Chartres grew from a civic twinning between the two see cities, inaugurated in 1959, which soon involved a link between the two

---

[12]   *Twinnings and Exchanges. Jumelages et Echanges (op. cit.).* See also R. Blount, *European Church Partnership* (CAFE, Cambridge, 1994).

Mgr Perrier, Bishop of Chartres, blesses a set of vestments presented to his cathedral by Canon Greenacre. They were a gift from the Bishop, Diocese and Cathedral of Chichester to mark the 800th anniversary of the beginning of the rebuilding of Chartres Cathedral after the disastrous fire of June 1194.

cathedrals. The roots of the link between Canterbury and Arras (which are neighbouring dioceses) lie in the attendance of Bernard Pawley, a future Archdeacon of Canterbury, as an Anglican observer at the Second Vatican Council. The first *grande rencontre* between the two dioceses was held in 1975. The Bristol-Bordeaux link began in 1979, and involves members of the *Eglise Réformée* (unusually for France, 12-15% of the population of Bordeaux are Reformed). Twinnings at diocesan level have continued to increase in number. Two further links were established during the later 1980s – between Salisbury and Evreux and between Truro and Quimper et Léon. The latter is not specifically a diocesan link; it centres on the Breton Abbey of St-Guenolé (St Winwaloe) in Landevennec, and is a link between Christians of all denominations in Cornwall and Christians (mostly, but not exclusively, Catholic) in Brittany. To these links at diocesan level must be added the twinning between Manchester and Toulouse, which began in 1969. The link focuses on Manchester Cathedral and the Church of St Sernin, Toulouse, but most of the Toulouse members of the Twinning Association (which is the main focus for Catholic-Reformed relations in Toulouse) worship in other churches, as do quite a proportion of the Manchester members. There are also, of course, other cathedral links, such as that between Winchester Cathedral and the Abbey of St-Benoît-sur-Loire (Fleury).

Alongside the phenomenon of twinning there has been another more personal kind of link; the increasing number of inter-church marriages (*foyers mixtes*) involving Anglicans and French Catholics and calling for the co-operation of Anglican and French Catholic clergy in preparing the couples for their marriage and in devising a wedding ceremony that finds place for two languages and two rites. The 'French connection'– the whole network of close links between Anglicans in Great Britain and Catholics in France, with its deep historical roots and wider ramifications – finds a particular kind of sacramental earthing in such interchurch marriages, which plead for an *entente cordiale* between two nations and the recovery of unity between two churches.

A Mutual Attraction

Anglicans are drawn to French Catholicism by the imaginitive freedom and openness they have discovered in its pastoral and missionary initiatives and in its theological and liturgical thinking. In the field of liturgy they have learned not only from the scholars but also from some of the experiments in pastoral liturgy which anticipated the reforms of the Second Vatican Council by some years. They have also realized that the French Church's strong and deeply rooted conviction of the necessity of being in communion with the Roman See does not inhibit French Catholics from being ready on occasion to criticize the particular ways in which the Roman primacy is currently exercised. French Catholic interest in Anglicanism has many nuances. There is first of all the fascination

Choristers from Chartres with the choir of Chichester Cathedral in the Song School at Chichester, June 1995

of a tradition that is in such marked contrast to French Protestantism and to the *Eglise Réformée de France* in particular. There have been remarkable achievements in Catholic-Protestant dialogue in France; some of the work of the pioneering *Groupe des Dombes* has been seen as particularly significant by the Church of England's Faith and Order Advisory Group. Nevertheless, French Catholics have constantly stressed the importance of Orthodox and Anglican involvement in the dialogue in order to broaden the horizon and to avoid certain impasses. Though the main work of French ARC has been concerned with relations between the two churches in France itself, the need for making Anglicanism better known in France and diffusing better and more accurate information about it in French has been an important part of its agenda. Interest in Anglicanism on the part of French Catholics has by no means been confined to those of a liberal or radical tendency; many of those in a more conservative tradition have also been looking sympathetically at Anglican experience and particularly at the Anglican liturgical tradition. In the immediate aftermath of Vatican II French Catholicism seemed to be polarized into two extremes; a rigidly conservative tendency which looked to Archbishop Lefebvre for inspiration and a 'modern' tendency which could be impatiently dismissive of the recent past and in its haste to change everything both pastorally insensitive and destructive of much that was worth retaining. French Catholics who were distressed by this polarization looked to Anglicans to see how 'pluralism', which was now held up before them as an ideal but of which they had little practical experience, could work out in practice, how a musical tradition could cope with the introduction of the vernacular and how liturgy could be at the same time both dignified and traditional and also open to change and reform. Anglicans sometimes needed to remind French Catholics at that time of their own painful experience in the sixteenth century, of the danger of throwing out the baby with the bath water and of the difficulty of trying to revive a tradition once it had been discarded.[13]

English Roman Catholic Involvement

Finally, it is necessary to record one fundamental change that has radically affected the character of this 'French connection' without however making it redundant. From the seventeenth century until the Second Vatican Council the principal reason why Anglicans cultivated ecumenical relations with French and Belgian Catholics was that they were conscious that – with some notable exceptions – they would not find the same sympathy and interest among English Roman Catholics. To understand this, Anglicans have only to reflect with more penitent awareness on the history of persecution experienced over many centuries by the Recusant minority in England.

It is also important to point out – though lack of space does not allow this to be done in any detail – that there is a long history of close contact and mutual support between

---

13   In a conversation recorded in *Fifty Years of Catholic Theology. Conversations with Yves Congar,* ed. B. Lauret (London, 1988), Yves Congar referred with cautious approval to the use of the phrase 'deforestation' to describe the effects of the post-conciliar radical agenda on popular religious practice in France.

English and French Roman Catholics, with English seminaries and religious houses located in France until the French Revolution and French Catholics playing a notable role in the 'Second Spring' of English Roman Catholicism after that Revolution, and particularly when the religious orders were expelled from France and many of them found refuge in England.

During the debates at the Second Vatican Council on the Decree on Ecumenism in 1963 it is remarkable that among those who pleaded for some special mention to be made of Anglicanism were two French bishops (Cardinal Gouyon of Rennes and Bishop Collin of Digne) and the Bishop of Monaco, Jean Rupp. They were joined by a bishop from South Africa, who pleaded for a re-examination of Anglican Orders, and the English and ex-Anglican Abbot of Downside, Dom (later Bishop) Christopher Butler. Archbishop (later Cardinal) Heenan, while committing the Roman Catholic Church in England to full and wholehearted participation in ecumenical dialogue, could not resist an implicit criticism of the French and Belgians when he asked the Council to recommend that normally the dialogue should be carried on in the countries where Christians of the traditions involved were living side by side.

Even in the post-conciliar period there have been tensions between English and French Roman Catholics over relations with Anglicans, the English suspecting the French of an over-optimistic and unrealistic assessment of Anglicanism and the French suspecting the English of narrowness and an inability to free themselves from the consequences of past hostility and bitterness. More recently, however, the vital contribution of English Roman Catholics to the ARCIC dialogue and close collaboration between the national Anglican - Roman Catholic Committees of England, France and Belgium have begun to change these perceptions. It is not without significance that one of the most positive of the responses issued by Episcopal Conferences to the *Final Report* of ARCIC I was that of the Bishops of England and Wales in 1985. It is no less significant that the bodies which have replaced the old British Council of Churches have had the kind of structure which has enabled the Roman Catholic Church to become a full member of, for example, Churches Together in England and to be in the forefront of co-operation in mission and service at every level from the very small, very local and informal to that of bishops and church leaders. It is not that the special relationships between English Anglicans and Continental Roman Catholics can now be discarded; it is rather that they must not be used as an excuse for ignoring relationships at home.

As Dr John Habgood, Archbishop of York, said in a sermon in York Minister in 1984 to commemorate the 50th anniversary of the death of Lord Halifax,

> Sometimes those who are close to one another find it hard to break away
> from stereotyped responses, especially where there are hundreds of years
> of history which have to be reckoned with, and forgiven. And so to start
> at all we have to start a bit further away from home. The vision has to be
> widened if it is not to be blocked by the painful experiences and memo-
> ries of the past. And if friendship between an English Viscount, a French
> priest and a Belgian Cardinal is needed to get it going, then this is all part

of the pattern of God's working – to take us out of ourselves, and then send us home again with a vision which embraces the world.

But now, all these decades later, the question comes back at us – what have we done at home? How far has this friendship between our dioceses been used to stimulate and encourage relationships between our Churches in our own countries?[14]

The Abbey of Bec

Visitors from England, especially if they land at Dieppe, Le Havre or Caen, can quickly and easily reach the Norman village of Le Bec-Hellouin in the lovely and peaceful valley of the stream called *Le Bec* and there find the great Abbey of Notre-Dame du Bec-Hellouin. It was here that this chapter began, and here it should end, for Bec has served not only as a symbol, but also as a focus, of relations between the English and French churches.

The monastery was founded in 1034 by a former knight called Herluin (from whom abbey and village take their name). Its beginnings were poor and obscure; its fame was due to two recruits from the north of Italy – Lanfranc (from Pavia) and Anselm (from Aosta). Lanfranc was not only endowed with a brilliant intellect but also with the gift of being an inspiring teacher; during his time in the monastery the School of Bec attracted pupils from all over the western world. William the Conqueror made him the first Abbot of his new foundation of St-Etienne (the *Abbaye aux hommes*) at Caen and then, in 1070, Archbishop of Canterbury. Lanfranc's successor as Prior and Herluin's as Abbot was St Anselm, perhaps the greatest and most attractive churchman of his time and one who has had a profound and enduring influence on Christian theology and spirituality to this day. He was to succeed Lanfranc as Archbishop of Canterbury in 1093 and to die there in 1109. In 1930 a plaque was set up on the Abbey's Tour St-Nicolas by some English donors 'to commemorate the close links which united the former Abbey of Le Bec-Herluin and the Church of England in the 11th and 12th centuries, when three of the sons of this Abbey occupied the Primatial See of Canterbury, three became Bishops of Rochester and several others ruled as abbots of important religious houses'. To this day place names like Tooting Bec serve as reminders of the many properties given to the Abbey in England.

The Abbey experienced periods of decline, suffering both from the Hundred Years' War and the Wars of Religion and also from the imposition of commendatory abbots after the concordat of 1516. It had a considerable renewal of vitality when it was taken in hand by the reforming congregation of St-Maur in the seventeenth century; it is to the Maurists that we owe the magnificent conventual buildings of the seventeenth and eighteenth centuries, now restored to their former glory. But the French Revolution wrought the Abbey's ruin; in 1792 the last monks were forced to leave and some years later the church was demol-

---

[14]   Cf. *One in Christ*, xx (1984), p.155.

ished. The monastic buildings were handed over to the army and for long served as a cavalry remount depot, with the cloisters converted into stables. The Abbey is still the property of the State, but in 1948 it became once again a Benedictine monastery.

The community which came to Bec was founded by Père Emmanuel André, who died in 1903, at Le Mesnil-Saint-Loup in Champagne; the greater part of it was at the time of the move at Cormeilles-en-Parisis on the outskirts of Paris. There a priory of monks had been established alongside the house of the 'moniales-oblates' of St Frances of Rome – the sisters are known technically as 'moniales-oblates' rather than nuns in order to be free from strict enclosure. The two communities, which belong to the Olivetan Congregation (one of whose distinguishing marks is that the monks wear a white rather than a black habit) were in very close relationship, particularly in the celebration of the liturgy. The move to Bec was led by the Prior, Dom Paul Grammont, soon to become the 46th Abbot of Bec and first Abbot of the new foundation. The sisters followed the community of monks to Bec after a short delay and built their own convent – the *Monastère Sainte-Françoise-Romaine* – nearby. More recently the Abbey of Bec has restored the monastery of Le Mesnil-Saint-Loup and established a monastery at Abu-Gosh near Jerusalem (at both of which places can be found both monks and sisters); there was also for some years a small foundation in Northern Ireland near Belfast.

The kiss of peace of two successors of St Anselm. The Abbot of Bec (Dom Paul Grammont) welcomes the Archbishop of Canterbury (Dr Michael Ramsey) to his Abbey for the First Vespers of St Anselm in April 1967.

The two communities had a strong ecumenical orientation even before the move to Bec; Dom Emmanuel had begun to take an interest in the Eastern Churches as early as 1883, while Dom Lambert Beauduin – in exile from Chevetogne – was for a time chaplain to the sisters at Cormeilles-en-Parisis. Part of the attraction that drew the community to Bec was the spiritual tradition of St Anselm and the call to build on that tradition by establishing links with Anglicanism. Even on the day of the 'Return', Michaelmas Day 1948, a few Anglicans were invited to the ceremony, including Fr Geoffrey Curtis CR and the Revd Charles Neate, Chaplain of St George's, Paris. From that time friendly relations with Anglicans were pursued, although during the years preceding the Council this policy was not without its risks and did attract for a time some hostility from the Roman Catholic hierarchy in England. The kiss of peace was given very publicly when Cardinal Heenan presided over the mass at the consecration of the new Abbey Church (formerly the refectory) in 1969. Bec now welcomes many Anglican pilgrims – both individuals and groups from parishes and university chaplaincies. History was made on the Feast of St Anselm in 1967 when Dr Michael Ramsey, Archbishop of Canterbury, was given a solemn liturgical reception at the Abbey and the two successors of St Anselm, Archbishop and Abbot, both in cope and mitre, presided together at the First Vespers of the Feast and gave the blessing together from the High Altar. During this visit Dr Ramsey decorated both Abbot Paul and the then Prior (and present Abbot), Dom Philibert Zobel, with the Cross of St Augustine. A very strong relationship has grown up from that day between the Diocese and Cathedral of Canterbury and the Abbey of Bec, and it is symbolized at Bec by the Cross of Canterbury which was set into the wall of the Abbey Church at the time of its consecration with this inscription:

> La Cathédrale de Cantorbéry à l'Abbaye du Bec-Herluin
> en communion de destin et d'espérance
> [From the Cathedral of Canterbury to the Abbey of
> Le Bec-Herluin in communion of destiny and hope]
> Ut omnes unum sint. I.XI.MCMLXIX.

AFTERWORD

I am grateful for the opportunity to welcome Roger Greenacre's book and in doing so to thank him for his own contribution over many years to the life of our own church in France and to relations with the Roman Catholic Church of the country. Much of what I would like to write he has already said in the text. My particular concern is to acknowledge with gratitude the friendship with which our priests and congregations (and indeed their bishops) are received by our Roman Catholic brothers and sisters. Hospitality, whether in invitations to use church buildings, or, in the absence of an Anglican priest, to share in the Eucharist, is much appreciated. Many members of 'satellite' congregations which only occasionally have an Anglican service enjoy already a kind of double-fellowship, glad to retain their own Anglican identity but at the same time to share with their Roman Catholic neighbours in the life of the parish church the rest of the time. My prayer is that as time goes on our newer friendship with the French Protestant churches will bear similar fruit and that we will be able to look forward with even greater confidence to the common future God has promised.

✠ JOHN HIND
Bishop in Europe

15 September 1995

USEFUL ADDRESSES

Twinnings and Exchanges / Jumelages et Echanges is available from the Council for Christian Unity, Church House, Great Smith Street, London SW1P 3NZ at £1.50 + 35p p and p.

Information about Anglican chaplaincies in France is available from the Diocesan Office of the Diocese in Europe, 14 Tufton Street, London SW1P 3QZ, tel: 0171-976 8001, fax: 0171-976 8002.

The address of the Ecumenical Secretariat of the French Bishops' Conference is:

La Commission Episcopale pour l'Unité des Chrétiens
80, rue de l'Abbé Carton   Tel: (1) 45 42 00 39
75014 PARIS   Fax: (1) 45 42 03 07